Confessions of an Aging Beauty Queen

A Comedic Guide to Pageantry

MONICA SKYLLING

Confessions of an Aging Beauty Queen

Copyright © 2019 by Pensiero Press

All rights reserved. No part of this book may be reproduced or transmitted in any form or by any means, graphic, electronic or mechanical, including photocopying, recording, taping, Web distribution, or by any informational storage and retrieval system without written permission from the publisher except for the inclusion of brief quotations in a review or scholarly reference.

Books are available through Pensiero Press at special discounts for bulk purchases for the purpose of sales promotion, seminar attendance, or educational purposes. Special volumes can be created for specific purposes and to organizational specifications. Please contact us for further details.

ISBN: 978-1-73293-825-0
*Kindle and electronic versions available

Please note that things learned in this book are not a guarantee of future performance, such as top placement in the finals or a pageant winner.

All photos courtesy of Monica Skylling's personal collection.

Cover design and interior by Gary Rosenberg

Printed in the United States of America

10   9   8   7   6   5   4   3   2   1

Contents

Testimonials v

Foreword xi

Acknowledgments xv

Prologue xvii

~ PART I ~

CHAPTER 1 My Story 1

CHAPTER 2 Mrs. Illinois-America 1990 9

CHAPTER 3 Mrs. Illinois-America 1991 20

CHAPTER 4 Mrs. Illinois-America 1992 30

CHAPTER 5 When Things Go Wrong—Take 1 46

CHAPTER 6 Ms. Illinois 1995 49

CHAPTER 7 Mrs. Illinois-America 1997 53

CHAPTER 8 When Things Go Wrong—Take 2 56

CHAPTER 9 Mrs. Illinois-America 1999 61

CHAPTER 10 When Things Go REALLY Wrong 72

CHAPTER 11 Mrs. America 77

CHAPTER 12 Coaching 93

CHAPTER 13 Competing in the Latter Years 97

CHAPTER 14 Not All Pageants Are Alike 110

~ PART II ~

Getting Ready 115

Paperwork 117

Interview 122

State Costume 140

Swimsuit/Fitness Wear 146

Evening Gown 152

Miscellaneous Tips 156

Packing List 166

In Closing 171

About the Author . . . 173

Testimonials

Clarissa Burt

CEO/Founder of *The EnvelopHer.com* Movement
Women's Advocate and Leader for Social Change
https://clarissaburt.com/

Monica offers a comedic perspective on her amazing journey as a pageant queen. This is a must read for those who want to compete in pageants—regardless of age. Who better to have as a coach than someone who has already found success winning 4 crowns and pageant titles? Everyone who competes in a pageant should add this to their library to help them In the LimeLight (podcast with Clarissa Burt).

James K. Gibson

Managing Partner
The Gibson Organization LLC
https://www.facebook.com/TheGibsonOrganization/

As the former Director of Pageant Affairs for the Miss Universe Organization, I've hosted more than 1,500 Pageant telecasts and/or specials over the past 40 years. I've seen the positive influence pageantry has brought to millions of women across the globe. My stages have graced over 100,000 contestants including Halle Berry, Vanna White, and Monica Skylling. I am excited to see that Monica has written an excellent book. I would encourage anyone to read her book and learn from her experiences which is the best way to approach pageantry and succeed.

Bonnie Bonadeo

The Connection Coach Speaker
Coach, Author, Audio Influencer-Podcaster
http://www.BonnieBonadeo.com

I admire the courage of women to put themselves out there at any age and believe there should be no age limit placed on beauty queens. Monica's journey was more about her own empowerment and the sisterhood of other women even though they were competing against each other and less about winning a beauty competition. In essence, the competition was really about finding and loving herself.

Iris Echevarria

Flight Attendant
American Airlines

Having *Confessions of an Aging Beauty Queen* before my Flight Attendant interview would have been a game changer! There are so many interview tips and guides that can help you prepare and ace an important interview in ANY field! The positive messages sprinkled throughout this book will empower you to go for your goals and get that dream job, which makes this a must-read for ANYONE!

*This book is lovingly dedicated to all
current and future pageant contestants,
especially those who are just beginning their
journey as I did over 30 years ago. May my
words help guide you down all the roads
to success that you are dreaming about.*

Foreword
by JoAnn Fakhouri

I REMEMBER GROWING UP as a little girl, sitting in the family room with my parents and siblings, watching the beauty pageants on our television set. I admired those beautiful women wearing sparkling gowns, all dolled up. As we anxiously waited to find out who would be crowned the next Miss America or Miss USA, I often wondered what motivated those women to participate in the pageants. Were they driven by vanity or some other force?

The answer to that question became apparent in 2012 when I was asked by Michael Galanes to judge the Little Miss Perfect Pageant. During that competition, I had an opportunity to ask an eight-year-old contestant why it was important for her to be crowned the next Little Miss Perfect. As she looked down with sadness in her eyes, she replied, "So people will see me as pretty." I was stunned by her response, reinforcing how beautiful she actually was. Then she continued with her answer . . . "No, the kids at school say I'm not pretty and they make jokes about me. At least if they see me on stage, they may view me differently."

At that moment, I realized the pageants do not exist for the purpose of getting people to like you through competition, but rather to build your self-esteem so that you gain the strength to stand up to the bullies who exist in our communities. I certainly hope that little girl found the confidence and voice she was searching for.

I was drawn by the lure of the lights and cameras when I originally started in the industry. I modeled and acted for many years and appeared in magazines, television commercials and movies. However, I eventually realized the power of working behind the camera. Through production, I could influence a larger audience and change perceptions on issues that have a greater impact on society, i.e., diversity and human trafficking.

As I read Monica's book, the landscape of media she wrote about was so powerful that I was able to identify with the experiences Monica so candidly depicted. The power of the media and choosing to be in the spotlight is a mixed blessing. I admire Monica's resilience during her entire career in this field. The highs and lows are equally portrayed, and the reality of the process is clearly revealed. I respect that she has chosen to help others through her experiences. Let's face it, being a strong, independent woman in this day and age is something we all should be proud of. Stereotypes and preconceived notions are no longer acceptable, no longer welcome.

After working in the film industry for over 20 years, I proudly opened Capital J Productions, my own production company and PR firm. I feel this was a great accomplishment for me as a woman, seeing how female roles as producers, and especially directors, were limited. I have produced and directed films, commercials, music videos and so much more for my clients, helping them achieve their dreams and goals. That is a wonderful feeling. It's not always about ourselves, but rather helping others achieve their goals as well.

Monica refers to her struggle with weight and I, too, struggled. It became a problem as I grew older, which eventually led to many food sensitivities. I eventually created a gluten-free, dairy-free and vegan cheesecake called *The Best F*ing Cheesecake Ever*! This creation was one of the semi-finalist winners as PeaPods' Next Best Product and was featured on *Windy City Live*. This product will revolutionize cheesecake lovers' palettes. Visit **www.freeingsweets.com**

Congratulations, Monica, on living your life with purpose and drive. Congratulations also for helping inspire others who look to you as a role model, whether it be your children, future Pageant contestants or simply any young or adult female who picks up this book. Dreams are a GIFT from God. It is our choice whether we choose to follow them. I hope you continue to realize your dreams!

Kindest Regards,
JoAnn

JoAnn Fakhouri is Producer, Public Relations, and Director at Capital J Productions, LLC

Mobile: **708-691-4461**

E-mail: **joannfakhouri@yahoo.com**

Website: **www.capitaljproductions.com**

Pageants judged:

- 2013 Miss Illinois-USA Pageant
- 2014 Miss Illinois-USA Pageant
- 2015 Miss Assyrian Pageant
- 2012 American COEd Pageant
- 2012 Little Miss Perfect Pageant

Acknowledgments

As with any book that is written, there are always many people to thank. Let me first start by thanking the people who have suggested I do this in the first place. It is one thing to live through certain experiences and think they are just normal, but it is another thing completely to hear other people outside of the pageant world laughing and telling you, you NEED to write a book! I thank you all for giving me the inspiration to do this.

Thank you also to all of the coaches, trainers, hair stylists, make-up artists, photographers, nail techs, old friends, new friends (especially my new SUPER supportive friend, Iris), roommates, directors, and sponsors (the list goes on and on) who have helped me throughout the years. EVERYONE is needed to get someone pageant ready.

To my family . . . thank you for all of your love and support. I don't know of too many people who could shop for hours on end, help me find the "perfect" dress (even though SEVERAL were almost perfect), help carry my bags and do it with a smile on your face the entire time!

To my photography "Dream Team" . . . Daniel DuVerney, Jonathan Abernathy, and Triphena Johnson, you all saw my vision and helped me capture the PERFECT shot for the cover photo and I can't thank you enough!

My attorney, Vic Ciradelli . . . thank you so much for all you have done to help me both in the past and in the present. Your talents will certainly be missed by the entire city of Chicago should you ever decide to retire (but you probably won't)!

Lastly . . . to my oldest and dearest BFFs, Lisa and Jeanne. You have stood by my side, helped me prepare and cheered me on through (almost) this entire journey. Had I met you both sooner, you would have been there from day one. Anyone would be lucky to have one friend like you, but somehow I have been blessed with two. I don't know what made me so lucky, but I'm truly thankful.

I hope you all enjoy reading my words as much as I have enjoyed writing them. May you all be blessed with dreams and goals . . . no matter what your age!

Prologue

SOMETIMES IN LIFE, IT IS IMPORTANT to step out of your comfort zone; a few years ago my husband suggested that I compete in another pageant. I looked at him and said, "I'm almost 50 years old!"

His answer was simple . . . "SO?"

I realized that he was right. SO WHAT that I'm almost 50! Is volunteering for your favorite charity different for a 50 year old than a 25 year old? Is it a bad idea to eat right and get into great shape at any age? I know that many people will laugh at me and think I'm crazy but honestly, those are the people who don't know what pageants are all about. Pageants are about doing great things in your community, taking good care of yourself and if applicable, showing your kids that just because you are getting older, it doesn't mean you need to stop having dreams and/or stop taking care of yourself.

Preparing for a pageant teaches you how to be the best *you* you can be. It teaches you how to work hard both mentally and physically while obtaining your goals. You become a master at juggling family, work and pageant prep and think it is insanely FUN! I challenge anyone to say that any of these things are *bad* for a 50-year-old! So, I once again threw my hat in the ring and competed in a large national pageant against women half my age . . . and I couldn't be more proud!

A few years ago it was suggested to me that I write a book about my 30+ year pageant history. This person was the director of a musical I was performing in and she thoroughly enjoyed hearing all the behind the scenes action. It was brought to my attention, once again by somebody else that I put my experiences down on paper.

I hope that my quirky personality comes across in my writing. I intentionally wrote this book in a style similar to two friends chatting it up over a cup of coffee, because let's face it . . . coffee talk RULES!

I suppose that I have often felt that my life experiences are just *normal*. However, when I say them out loud or write them down, I realize that they are anything but!

Competing in pageants for so many years has taught me many things, including:

- Surviving on egg whites and Tic Tac's is NOT a good idea! (I always ate relatively normal.)
- Everyone is NOT your best friend.
- Your best friends CAN be made through pageantry!

Also . . .

- Did you know that Preparation H has more than one function?
- Or that Vaseline and Firmgrip are invaluable in a pageant dressing room?

Prologue

- Better yet . . . what could 50 beauty queens be doing backstage lined up, topless, waiting for their turn with a chaperone?

For the answers to these questions (and more), keep turning the pages!

~*Monica*

CHAPTER 1
My Story

MY PAGEANT STORY DID NOT START as a child. I was not involved in anything like the show *Toddlers and Tiaras*, nor did I know that pageants for children even existed. I did, however, always want to be involved in the entertainment industry. My Swedish parents did not share or understand my passion, which unfortunately resulted in often being told *no*.

I remember as a 3 or 4 year old asking to be in commercials, but I was told no. Again as a high school student I asked to go to modeling school, but I was told no. My parents were not mean in any way; they just did not understand. As soon as I turned 18, I signed myself up for modeling school at a local agency. *Fashionating Images* would change the course of my life.

Being a first generation born American, I always felt that it was important to become successful in this *land of opportunity* that my Dad dreamed about. My brothers were born in Sweden, but I was born here in America. We moved back to Sweden when I was 5 years old but came back a few years later.

Those few years were very impressionable for me. I loved having extended family all around and was less than happy to leave them behind when we came back to

America. School was very difficult as I forgot my English during those years. Kids can be very mean, and I was bullied for not being able to understand them. I was bullied and teased in junior high school again for various reasons.

One time I remember clearly being bullied for a pair of shoes. Clogs were the latest fashion trend in this country and my aunt had sent my mom and me each a pair from Sweden. I was so proud to wear my new Swedish *Träskor* to school the next day. To my amazement and horror, I was teased relentlessly because they were blue. I never wore them to school again.

Teasing and bullying didn't stop in high school, but my overall experience was much better. I made some amazing friends in band and also some good ones as a cheerleader. I didn't realize it then, but as an adult I realized just how low my self-esteem was during those years. I remember not trying out for the freshman cheerleading squad because in my mind I was thinking *"Why bother . . . I won't make it anyway."* Sophomore year wasn't much better, but I drummed up the nerve to at least try out. I didn't "check off the box" for sophomore squad for the same reason as the year before, but I did try out for the *less desirable* JV squad. To my amazement . . . I made it! I had a great year and by the time I was a senior, I was captain of the varsity squad!

Band, however, was my life in high school and I am still friends with these people today. My band friends are very much like my pageant friends. They never bullied or teased anyone; everyone was accepted for who they were and most important, they ALWAYS had your back!

Graduation was bittersweet. I knew I would miss band,

My Story

but I was excited for what the world had to offer! Being that my parents weren't from this country, college was always an option but not a requirement. It was instilled upon my brothers and I that you could fare just as well by being good at a specific trade. I had planned on taking a year off and then going to college, but after visiting some friends at the University of Illinois who took me to some frat parties, I decided that college was not for me.

Shortly after graduation, I signed myself up for modeling school just like I dreamed about. It wasn't one of the big, famous chain schools, but I learned things that I use and think about to this day. I would highly recommend a school like this for any teenage girl, even if she doesn't have any aspirations of being a model. The things I learned about skin care, make-up, and basic etiquette are things that I will carry with me for the rest of my life. It wasn't long until the school's agency started booking me for modeling jobs. It took even less time for me to realize that I was hooked!

The modeling world was exciting! I loved it all! Print shoots were fun (my agency even began using my photos for their brochure) and so were fashion shows! The fashion shows created quite a dilemma for me though, because I am SHORT! There is a reason why models are tall. Clothes used in fashion shows are generally samples which are made for taller people, not for someone 5'5" (5'4½" if you want to get technical!). Pretty much everything I had to wear was too long. I knew that I would never be a supermodel and I was ok with that. I also knew it was possible to have a successful career anyway.

After a year or so, my agent presented another opportunity to me. She suggested that I compete in the Miss Northwest Communities Pageant. This was a preliminary in the Miss America system.

"Um . . . YES! Where do I sign up??!"

I admittedly knew NOTHING about pageants other than what I had seen on TV. Again, since my parents didn't understand my passion, I couldn't count on support from them, so I sought assistance on my own.

Because this was my first pageant, I didn't know that pageant coaches existed. Since this was in 1984, I didn't have videos to watch to help me prepare. I was pretty much on my own.

I didn't want to wear my old prom dress and I didn't have any money to buy a new one. Luckily, a mom at the daycare center where I worked said she had a bridesmaid dress that she could lend me. It was lovely! It wasn't a pageant gown by any stretch of the imagination, but when I put it on, I felt pretty and that's the most important thing.

As for the talent portion, a friend of mine and I used to choreograph dance routines just for fun; she helped me put together a rousing routine to *One Night in Bangkok*. I wore a swimsuit that I had at home because I didn't know it had to be much better than that. Most important, I didn't have any help preparing for the interview nor did I understand just how important the interview was,

ESPECIALLY in the Miss America system! I was as ready as I was going to be. The pageant came and I was clearly out of my league! I felt very young.

There were two girls who stood out above everyone else. One of them was very sweet and told me that she would love

to see me back in a few years after I gained some experience. The other was a doll with the voice of an angel! She went on to win and later became First Runner-Up to Miss Illinois! *I think she should have been Miss America, but that's just my opinion.* I felt that I did the best I could, and you can't ask for more than that. Even though I did not place, I knew that I couldn't wait to do it again the next year!

The next year's preparation went about the same as the previous year. The pageant referred me to someone who lent out dresses to the girls who couldn't afford to buy one. The one I got was HIDEOUS! I honestly would have been better off in my old prom dress. I should have gone that route because I didn't feel pretty AT ALL! I wore the same swimsuit as the previous year, but again, without a coach, there was no one to tell me that polka dots and ruffles were not pageant appropriate. I did, however change my talent. I played *In the Mood* by Glenn Miller on my saxophone and felt very good about my performance. Again, there was no one to tell me how important the interview portion was to this competition. In two words . . . I TANKED!

After the pageant, I was given feedback that my talent was one of the highest scores in the competition but that I needed to lose weight. WHY DIDN'T ANYONE TELL ME TO GET HELP WITH THE INTERVIEW? I would find out later that the Miss America Organization has one of the toughest interviews in any pageant system on the planet! A heads up on this subject would have been helpful! Oh well, live and learn.

During this time I also did one of the most fun things in my life up until then. I took classes at *The Player's Workshop of the Second City*! It was a HOOT! I only took one semester, but it was AMAZING to take improv in Chicago, the city that put improv on the map! It would take 20 years, but I would return to this later.

My agent also put me in touch with another photographer where we shot the photos for my first modeling composite. It was a very exciting time, to stay the least!

My Story

In 1986, I decided to move back to Sweden for a time to be with my extended family. While there, I was able to study acting, improv and voice at the Kulturama School for Performing Arts in Stockholm. This was and is still one of the top performing arts schools in the country and I was lucky to be there. I still remember the feelings that I had when I would walk the halls. It was magical! Walking by people in practice rooms, listening to them prepare their various talents, hearing the blend of all the different instruments and voices created an incredible mix of emotions. I felt like I belonged there.

This must be what people feel like when they are in college studying their passion. I really wish that I would have had more college guidance because I didn't understand that there

were majors available to me in the subjects I was interested in, like musical theater. I don't regret my choices in life, but I have and will always instill in my children the need to work toward their passion.

Shortly after I returned from Sweden in 1987, I became engaged. I later married in 1989 and this is where my pageant story really takes off.

CHAPTER 2
Mrs. Illinois-America 1990

IN 1988, I LANDED A DREAM JOB! I was hired by United Airlines. I started in Reservations but knew that after my obligatory one year of answering phones, the world would be my oyster! Six months later, I was married, and, thanks to my flight benefits, we had an amazing honeymoon!

A few months after settling into married life, I discovered an ad in the newspaper that would forever change me in ways I could only dream of at the time. The ad was searching for contestants for the upcoming **Mrs. Illinois-America Pageant**. **HOLD THE PHONE** . . . there is a **MRS.** America Pageant? I thought my pageant dreams were over once I got married. Could I be reading this correctly? Did it say Mrs., as in MARRIED? I had to call and find out more!

Sure enough, I had read correctly, and the paperwork was on its way. All I had to do was fill out the application, send in some pictures along with an application fee, and hope for the best. It seemed to take forever to find out if I would be selected as a contestant. The timing seemed to be perfect. I was older than when I had competed in the past, which equated to some life experience. I had been married long enough to be eligible. And, working the midnight shift at United threw my metabolism into a tailspin and I had lost a significant amount of weight, which is what the other pageant had suggested I do.

Now the waiting game began. It's funny how slowly time goes by while waiting for something good! Eventually the letter came, and I was accepted as a contestant! I was THRILLED! I didn't know it at the time, but most pageants are a business. Some will only accept a certain number of contestants. For the most part, you will not get turned away when there is a significant entry fee that each contestant must pay! Had I known that then, it would have taken some of the stress away, but in doing so, it would have also taken away some of the fun!

Now, here I am again. Back to square one . . . not knowing what to do! The directors of the Mrs. Illinois-America pageant were terrific about sending out information to help us prepare, but it still did not prepare me for what was to come.

The areas of competition were:

- Interview
- Swimsuit
- State Costume
- Evening Gown

Even though I now had a good job and my husband and I made decent money, I was still in the mindset of spending as little as possible. I used the same interview suit that I wore on my United Airlines interview. I again wore a swimsuit that I had at home and I went to my wedding photographer for a new headshot (I do not recommend doing this). I made my state costume (Monarch Butterfly—the Illinois State Insect) and my evening gown was purchased at a resale shop about 10 sizes too big. What was I thinking? I remember really liking the color but there were no sequins, no beads, and no bling WHATSOEVER! My mother-in-law was kind enough to take it in for me and it turned out quite nice for what it was. The gown fit me beautifully and I felt confident wearing it . . . until I got there.

I remember that orientation was very early in the morning. I had yet to discover the art of the *dry run* and my husband and I were completely lost! We couldn't find this hotel for anything! (Remember . . . no GPS yet). We drove up and down the same street for at least 45 minutes until we finally figured it out. I made it on time but just barely. I definitely did not need that added stress, but we got there in one piece and that's the important thing.

I remember sitting in orientation and feeling very small. I felt young and inexperienced. Some of these women seemed so elegant and I felt so out of place. We sat in orientation for a while and listened to some speeches from the director and the reigning winner. I was in awe. It felt so much different, so much bigger than the other pageants I had been involved in . . . and it was! I thought that since it was a *Mrs.* Pageant, the women wouldn't look like the *Miss* contestants on TV. They would be older, maybe a little heavier since many of them had children. It wouldn't be as *fancy* and *sparkly* as it is with the younger women. I couldn't have been more wrong! These women were in fantastic shape and there were more sequins and rhinestones than I had ever seen in one room in my life!

Uh oh!

The nerves were really kicking in!

Well, all I can do is my best and that is what I intended to do.

We were then whisked off to rehearse for the preliminary competition that evening. It would be held on a large stage in a beautiful venue. No hotel ballroom here! I can still feel the excitement of walking the stage while the opening number song was playing. (The song was *ESCAPADE* and I still break into my Pageant Walk when I hear it in a store)! We rehearsed for several hours. We had to learn:

- Opening number (State Costume)
- Swimsuit
- Evening Gown

Everybody competed in the preliminary competition, so everyone had to learn every number. It really wasn't that difficult once you learned the flow and figured out your assigned spot to stand on the stage. All the numbers were very similar, so it didn't seem that scary.

After rehearsals, we ate lunch and then were given a short amount of time to get ready for the all-important interview competition. This is where I bombed in the past, so I was really nervous! Pageant interviews are either a panel interview (5 judges sit across from the contestant, behind a conference table and take turns asking you questions for about 3–5 minutes) or one-on-one interview (the contestant spends about 5 minutes with each judge). The Mrs. Illinois-America interviews are a panel, which can be very intimidating, but it was the same in the other pageants I had competed in, so it was familiar. The only difference is that in this one, they wanted you to give a one minute speech telling the judges a little about yourself before they began asking questions.

While sitting outside the interview room waiting for your turn, you really have to make yourself stay focused. You will see women in some AMAZING interview suits and dresses, and you will begin second guessing your own. DON'T DO THAT! You chose your outfit for a reason. It made you feel pretty and confident. Don't second guess yourself. One rule of pageantry (and life) is that there will always be someone taller, thinner and prettier than you, but they are NOT you. Be the best *you,* you can be, and no one can compare with that!

It was now my turn, the dreaded interview. How will I make it through? To my surprise . . . just fine! My one minute speech went well, and I was thrilled to learn that this interview was NOTHING like my previous ones. This is where I learned that interviews differ between pageant systems. In *Miss America,* they ask a lot of current event and political questions. In *Mrs. America,* they want to learn about you. They ask you things on your bio. They ask about your family, your hobbies, and talents—things that you put on the application that you wanted them to know. Sometimes they asked about some other things, but it was still had to do with learning about you. Before I knew it, the bell rang, and my interview was over. How could that be? I wasn't done yet! I wanted to keep talking to them. They were so nice! I remember one of the judges was so very pretty. She sat in the center seat and smiled the whole time! She made me feel very comfortable. It turns out that she was a former winner and married to a Chicago Bear! She was my favorite.

After interviews were over, we were given dinner and some time to get ready for the preliminary competition that evening. My roommate was very sweet, and we got along great, so getting ready was fun! Before we knew it, it was time to board the bus to the theater.

Being backstage in a pageant dressing room is a very unique experience. I can honestly say that I saw things that I had never seen before. One of the girls walked around with a HUGE tub of Vaseline and people were gouging out huge chunks and spreading it across their TEETH! Eeeeewwww!!! Is that even safe? I was assured that it was safe, and it would help to prevent your lips from sticking to your teeth when you have to smile for an extended period of time. What the heck . . . I'll try it!

We were all ready to go in our costumes. The nerves were really starting to kick in. We were just waiting for the clock to strike 8:00 pm for the show to begin.

We were now brought to the wings of the stage. There were only a few moments to go and it would all begin. Our families and friends were in the audience waiting to cheer us on. It was exhilarating! Finally the music began, and we proceeded onto the stage in the opening number we were taught that morning. After that, we each took a turn at the microphone and introduced ourselves, as well as gave a brief description of our costume. You could definitely tell who was familiar with a microphone as those who were not, seemed a little terrified! Overall, it went well. I don't remember any major mishaps from anyone and that is always a good thing.

After the opening number, we were rushed downstairs to the dressing room to change into our swimsuits. This is where another unusual thing happened. The women were hiking up their swimsuits, giving themselves a major wedgie and having their butts sprayed! HUH? I was informed that it was *butt spray* and it made your cheeks *tacky* so that your suit wouldn't ride up on stage. Interesting. I would learn later that *butt spray* is not the technical term. It is actually called *Firmgrip,* which is what football players use to make their hands *tacky.* Who knew? I can tell you that it really does work! This is a good thing since picking out a wedgie on stage is a DEFINITE no no!

I have no memory of anything going wrong during this phase of competition. I was not particularly terrified as I was confident in my body and I felt that my swimsuit was fine. In retrospect, it probably wasn't as I was too skinny, and my swimsuit was not a *pageant* suit, but I didn't know any better at the time.

We were now rushed downstairs once again to change into our evening gowns. This is where I was not so confident. My mother-in-law did a beautiful job tailoring my dress to fit my body, but it was not even close to the caliber of gowns that were there that evening. I did the best I could but vowed to get a better gown if I ever did this again. My roommate told me that she thought my dress was "Simplistically beautiful," and that was a very kind thing to say! She was a sweet girl!

After the preliminary competition was over, we were

bussed back to the hotel for the Pageant Ball. This was a fun event for the whole family. It was an opportunity for the contestants to mingle but most important, it was a chance for the judges to mingle with the contestants and meet their husbands. Many other pageants do not agree with this philosophy. They keep the judges separated from the contestants at all costs. This one didn't. They must have felt that it was a good idea for the judges to see how the contestants interacted with their husbands. I can honestly say that if your husband is not very supportive of you, the judges will pick up on this and it could possibly hurt you in the competition. Maybe this is why they have the ball. It would be very tough on the directors to have a winner with a less than supportive husband. It would make for a very long year! All in all, the ball is a fun event. There was food, a cash bar and a DJ for lots of dancing. The contestants who  were *in it to win it* made their appearance and left early to get rest for the next day. The contestants who were *in it for fun* closed the place! It was a time to learn quite a bit about somebody.

    The next day was an all-day rehearsal and it began early! This is where going to bed at a decent hour the night before really paid off! We were once again bussed to the theater to rehearse for the final competition. This would be different than the day before because only the Top 10 would be competing. Since we didn't know who the Top 10 were going to be, we all had to practice making it.

The opening number would stay the same so that was just a quick run through. Then we had the *Parade of Beauty*, which meant that we all walked in very slowly in our evening gowns, in a particular order, and went to our *spot* on the stage. Then we all had to practice getting called into the Top 10 and then practice answering the dreaded onstage question.

We then had to practice the Top 10 swimsuit competition, which was different than the night before. Everyone had to practice walking out in a swimsuit wearing a fur coat, stopping center stage while you slipped the coat off into the hands of a U.S. Marine and then walking the runway. It was very different than the night before.

Evening gown would be different as well. You would walk out to the center stage and were met by a U.S. Marine who handed you a rose. Then you would be escorted to an archway made of swords which you would walk under to reach the runway. It was very elegant. Whoever was lucky enough to make the Top 10 would be in for an exciting evening.

Now we were bussed back to the hotel to get ready for finals. I had absolutely no idea what to expect. My placement (or lack thereof) in my previous pageants didn't allow me to hold out much hope, but this pageant was so much different. When we returned to the theater, all I could do was hope for the best.

Waiting in the wings for the show to start was much more nerve wracking than the night before. For those who didn't make the Top 10, they would be escorted to the balcony to watch the rest of the show. Their competition would be over. I wasn't ready for that. This was too much fun! I knew it would be over that evening either way, but I really wanted to compete one more time.

The opening number went well again and then we were brought back out to hear the results. After the emcee had said a few words and sang a lovely song, the moment arrived. (Fun fact-many years later, the emcee would end up playing the Wizard in the Chicago cast of *Wicked*).

The card was brought up onstage. The card with the names of the Top 10. I'm pretty sure the person next to me could hear my heart beating! He opened the envelope and began reading.

"The first Top 10 finalist in the Mrs. Illinois-America 1990 Pageant is . . . Monica Skylling!"

WHAAAAT???? I MADE IT!!!! I ACTUALLY MADE IT?!? I was in shock and SO excited! It was a wonderful moment. My roommate also made it, which made me very happy!

Now it was time for the onstage question. This is what will make or break many contestants. I know you have all seen botched answers on the Internet and now it would be time for mine. I actually did some preparation this time. The Miss USA Pageant had been on TV just 3 weeks before; I had written down all of their questions and gone over them in my head. I had also recorded the pageant and watched it several times. The question I got was:

"If the '80s were considered the *me* decade, what would you consider the '90s being?"

WHAAAAT??? They asked the same question at Miss USA! All I could hear in my head was what the Miss USA contestant had answered! I had watched the tape so many times that it was stuck in my brain! All I could do was to try and answer it differently and it came out all wrong. I blurted out something about the '90's being a *we* decade, which I think she said as well but I know my answer was at least a little different. Oh well, at least there was no YouTube back then. Now . . . on to swimsuit.

Here is where being called first really paid off! The Top 10 all had matching swimsuits, and we were able to pick between pink and blue and what size we wanted. Since I was called first, I got my pick of size and color! It was a MUCH nicer suit than the one I had worn the night before! Things were looking up! The fur coat I got to wear on stage was beautiful! You won't see that anymore today but in the '90s, it was very common.

Now, evening gown. Being escorted by a U.S. Marine and walking under the sword arch was incredible. It made me feel very special to have that opportunity and I had the pageant to thank for that. They put their heart and soul into this event, and it showed.

After evening gown, we were brought back onstage to be brought down to a Top 5. I didn't have much hope after my botched onstage question and rightfully so. I didn't make the cut, but I was TOTALLY ok with that! I had made the Top 10 and I was so proud! When I watched the Top 5 finish their competition, I was mesmerized. They were so beautiful, and I began to look at them as celebrities. I really didn't feel that I would have belonged in that group. The lady who won was as nice as she was beautiful, and I was proud to have been in the competition with her!

I couldn't wait to come back next year!

CHAPTER 3
Mrs. Illinois-America 1991

THE NEXT YEAR WAS SPENT WORKING hard at my career. My obligatory one year in Reservations had come to an end and I was able to transfer to the airport. I was now working as a Customer Service Representative (Ticket Agent) at O'Hare Airport in Chicago. I truly loved this job and made some lifelong friends during my time there. I was also pulled to work as a Concierge. An airline concierge would meet and assist celebrities and VIPs while at the airport. This was an amazing experience as I met many wonderful people and had some of my most embarrassing moments along the way.

One that I remember clearly was when I was supposed to meet Lester Holt. The manifest said that his assigned seat was 1B (aisle seat in First Class). I honestly thought that Lester Holt was an *older heavyset* gentleman with gray hair. When I boarded the flight, there was an *older heavyset* gentleman with gray hair in 1C (the opposite aisle seat in First Class). People change seats all the time, so I leaned over to him and said, "Mr. Holt?"

Lo and behold, I hear a voice behind me say . . . "Yes?"

I turned around and there is a young and very attractive

man, sitting in seat 1B smiling at me. He must have found humor in the fact that I obviously had NO idea who he was! Lester Holt is a very nice man!

As 1990 ended, my pageant preparations were in full swing. I sent in my application as soon as I could. In January of 1991, I received a phone call that would literally change my life. It's funny how such insignificant things can have such a huge impact.

The Director of the Pageant wanted to let me know that she saw *something* in me the previous year and she thought I would benefit from working with a pageant coach. Up until this point, I didn't know that pageant coaches existed. I was thrilled! She referred me to one of her former winners who had been very successful in coaching other contestants. My time working with her would change *everything I thought* I knew about pageants!

On my first visit to her house, she was on the phone when I arrived, and I was greeted by her husband. He was a very charming and outgoing man who proceeded to give me a tour of their home. They were in the process of having an indoor, inground pool installed and he informed me that there used to be batting cages in that spot. Who has batting cages IN their house? Apparently pro baseball players do. I had no idea, again who he was! I really do watch the news; I just seem to have a habit of meeting celebrities that I don't know!

His wife was a doll! We got along great and pageant coaching was one of the best experiences of my life! We worked on every aspect of competition. We worked on things that I never would have thought needed work! Here are some examples:

Pageant Walk: Different for each phase of competition

Pageant Stance: If it doesn't hurt, it doesn't work

Pageant Pivot: Kind of like Miss Congeniality, but not really

Interview:
- Choosing your interview suit
- How to enter the room
- How to sit
- When to sit
- Where to put your hands
- Where to put your feet
- How to construct your *One Minute Speech*
- The impact of the first word of your speech
- How to answer each question
- Where to look while answering each question
- How to end the interview when the bell rings
- How to exit gracefully

How to Choose a State Costume

Costume Introduction

How to Choose a Swimsuit
    How to walk and pivot in a swimsuit

How to Choose an Evening Gown
    How to walk and pivot in an evening gown

Onstage Question
    How to answer
    Where to look while you answer
    Where to look when you finish your answer

Hair and Makeup

    The majority of our time together we spent on the interview portion of the competition. In this pageant, the interview was 50% of the score. You have to do well to have any hopes of winning.

    Another thing that I learned during my training sessions was that everyone is NOT your friend. Up until this point, I had not had the pleasure of meeting a pageant *mean* girl, but my time was coming. More on that later.

    One very important aspect of training was that you have to be able to PICTURE yourself winning. She brought out her crown and we had a mock crowning. She announced me as Mrs. Illinois-America 1991 and placed the crown on my head! She also gave me a Polaroid photo of this moment and wanted me to PICTURE that moment in my mind every night before I went to sleep. How did the anticipation feel once the emcee received the envelope? What emotions was I feeling as my name was announced? How did it feel when the crown was slowly placed on my head? It was very strange doing this at first, but it is true, if you can't picture yourself winning, how can anyone else?

    During the few months we had before the pageant, my trainer and I became the best of friends. We spent many hours together working tirelessly in the short time we had before the pageant. One thing that she had me work on, that might be surprising to some of you, was my weight. I was too skinny! She had me drink a milkshake daily and always carry a Snickers bar in my purse. Knowing what I know today about healthy eating, this was probably not the best plan, but it worked.

She informed me that you usually lose about 5 pounds during the pageant weekend due to stress (my first introduction to *pageant diarrhea*); so her goal was for me to gain 5 pounds before the pageant so that I would stay the same. It was a tough job, but someone had to do it. I dutifully drank my daily milkshake and carried a Snickers bar with me wherever I went. Her plan worked as I didn't have any problem maintaining my weight during pageant weekend.

When the pageant weekend finally arrived, I felt ready, more than I ever could have imagined. I had a new headshot, I loved my interview suit and my trainer lent me the gown and swimsuit that she wore the year that she won. I felt incredible!

The events of the weekend went much the same as the year before. The only difference was that I was much more nervous. Feeling that I could actually win this thing put a whole other kind of pressure on me!

After a morning of rehearsals, it was time for the private interview. My trainer and I had worked so hard on my One Minute Speech that I knew exactly where to take each breath, as well as each hand gesture and eye movement. EVERYTHING was choreographed. (This may not work for some people, but it worked for me). Having acting experience made this easier for me than *winging* from an outline. The speech and interview went smoothly, and I felt confident in how I did. Funny how being prepared made me NOT dread the interview anymore. It actually became one of my favorite phases of competition!

Preliminaries went without a hitch. The only difference was that this year, the pageant was hosted by world famous pageant emcee and TV personality, Jim Gibson. Having him there gave the pageant a whole different feel, which would become evident the following evening.

The Pageant Ball was very similar to the previous year. You made your appearance, mingled a little with the judges, and off to bed!

The next day was spent at another long rehearsal. Once it was over, it was time for the final competition. I was covered in Vaseline, Aqua Net, and Firmgrip . . . I was ready!

The opening number was just as exciting as the previous year. As soon as the upbeat music started, my adrenaline went through the roof!

During the Parade of Beauty, I discovered how important it is to have an evening gown that makes you feel truly beautiful. I felt like I was floating across the stage. It doesn't have to cost a lot of money. In my case, it was borrowed (which is always smart to do, since pageants can become very costly).

I would also discover later that amazing gowns can be purchased in resale shops at a fraction of the cost. The most important thing is that the gown fits you properly and makes you feel beautiful.

Waiting onstage for the announcement of the Top 10 was very nerve wracking! All sorts of things were going through my mind. If I made it, I would at least do as well as the previous year. If I didn't make it, I would do worse.

If I made it; I would also have to answer the dreaded On Stage Question (which I bombed the previous year). But wait . . . I have had months of training! I know what I'm doing! Yay me!

The song had been sung, the speech had been made, and the host now had the envelope. Here we go . . .

"The first of our Top 10 finalists is" . . . *not me.*

Oh well, just because I was called first the previous year doesn't mean I would be called first again this year.

"The second finalist is . . . Monica Skylling!" *I MADE IT! WOO HOO!*

After watching the video tapes, I noticed something.

There were stars on the floor that the finalists were supposed to stand on. The first one called would go to the one farthest stage right. The second called would go to the one farthest stage left. Each subsequent finalist would alternate, working their way in towards the middle. What I noticed was that the shorter finalists were called first, and the taller ones called last. This made for a beautiful *arc* of women on stage during the interview portion. Very clever! Now I know why I was called first and second! I'm short! Not all pageants do this, so don't get discouraged if you are not called when you think you should!

Now it was time for the onstage interview. This is where it became evident that having a professional pageant host/emcee really makes a difference! There was absolutely nothing wrong with the previous year's host, but Jim made us ALL feel so comfortable. There was no *fishbowl* question. He had each of our bios and knew exactly what to ask to bring out the best in all of us. He was funny, kind and knew just how to work each person's interview to ensure that no one looked bad. It was honestly, almost magical to see. This is why he is still working successfully in this industry today and I am proud to call him and his wife my friend!

The Swimsuit competition felt very different than the previous year. I learned the *proper* pageant walk and pivot, had an AMAZING (and appropriate) pageant swimsuit and I felt like I knew what I was doing!

The Evening Gown portion also felt very different this year. I had no problem gliding across the stage in the most beautiful emerald green gown that I had ever seen. My new pageant walk made me feel confident and it showed.

Now it was time to call the Top 5 finalists. I didn't make the cut last year, but this year felt different. It was different because I was different and . . . I MADE IT! I made the Top 5!

Last year, I looked at these women as celebrities. I now realized then that they weren't celebrities at all. They were 5 women who had worked extremely hard to get to that point of the competition and they deserved to be there.

Now came the fun part. The emcee would bring up the Top 5 husbands to kill some time while the judges were tabulating. The husbands were made to walk the runway and were *judged* by the audience. This was a lot of fun and took some of the pressure off us while the judges were doing what they do. After the husbands returned to their seats, I saw that the judges were arguing. The host had to keep filling for time as the arguing continued. It seemed to take a very long time to get the results. I would find out later what happened.

Now the time was here:

4th Runner up is: . . . Not me

3rd Runner up is: . . . Not me

2nd Runner up is: . . . Not me

H@/Y CRAP! It's down to me and one other person. Training really does help! This is the moment that I had pictured in my mind every night for months! I couldn't believe it was actually happening!

1st Runner up is: . . . Me!

Huh? That's not how I pictured this moment . . .
Ok . . . hug the winner. Smile big. No boo-boo face allowed.
1st runner up is a GREAT accomplishment. Sometimes it just feels a little hard to come so close and yet . . . not close enough.
I would later hear rumors that the judges were arguing because there was a tie. What I heard was that half the judges wanted me, and half wanted her, and no one would budge. If this was true, I feel that in the end, they picked the right person. She was incredibly beautiful, kind, and was older than me and had kids. This was a *Mrs. Pageant* after all. Not that kids are necessary, but she had more life experience and I was only 25. Things always happen for a reason. I would find out later what my reason was for not winning that year.
Now I set my sights on next year!

CHAPTER 4

Mrs. Illinois-America 1992

THE NEXT YEAR WAS AGAIN SPENT working hard on my career. I truly loved working at the airport and had made some amazing, lifelong friends, but now I was now toying with the idea of becoming a Flight Attendant. Flying the Friendly Skies with United Airlines seemed like the next logical step in my career. At the beginning of the year, I submitted my transfer to In-Flight around the same time that I submitted my application to the Mrs. Illinois-America 1992 pageant. Now the waiting began!

Another fun thing that happened was that my trainer took me for some new headshots. She had also helped me get in touch with a new modeling agent, so we were able to take new photos with the amazing photographer, Rick Holz, for my modeling composite cards and portfolio as well. This was probably one of

the most fun photo shoots I have ever had! This photographer was amazing and one of the shots that I remember most was in Lake Michigan. Not AT Lake Michigan . . . IN Lake Michigan! He had me standing on some rocks and positioned just the right way so that the waves would crash under and between my legs. Every time the waves came in, I would get knocked over. Somehow I managed to keep my head above water to protect my make-up and in doing so, ironically the make-up artist had to keep spraying my hair with water to keep it wet. It took several tries until he got the perfect shot, but in the end . . . WE GOT IT! Needless to say, I came home with MANY bruises, but everyone was worth it as this turned out to be one of the coolest pictures I have from my early modeling days!

Training didn't really stop during that year. My trainer and I had become very good friends and we spent quite a bit of time together. The upcoming pageant was always on the back of my mind; planning and preparation always seemed to come up in conversation. One thing that would be different this year is that I would have new photos, a new interview suit, swimsuit and evening gown. Let the shopping begin!

Because I was so tiny, it was difficult finding a suit in my size. The *petite* stores didn't seem to have styles that I liked, so I resorted to finding a good seamstress instead. Stores usually only got one item in their smallest size, so I had to make sure to be at the right place at the right time.

I'll never forget the suit I ended up finding. It was navy, white and green and it was GORGEOUS! Believe it or not, I found it at Montgomery Ward's for $39! (See President Lincoln's Courtroom photo.) Once I had it tailored to my body, it looked like a million bucks! (This suit will come up again later in my story so keep it in mind!)

The swimsuit was easier to find. I don't remember the store, but I remember that it was black and gold and *very '90s*. It was chic, and I felt great wearing it.

Finding the evening gown was fun . . . fun . . . FUN! My trainer had a connection to a well-known designer whose warehouse is located outside of Chicago. We were able to go there and try on WHATEVER WE WANTED! It was amazing! I felt like a celebrity.

All the gowns were folded up in plastic, laying on shelves in a very organized fashion, like a library. I would just point at the ones I wanted to try on, and they pulled my size. Needless to say, we were there for HOURS!

I remember finding an absolutely AMAZING gown that was pink and fit me perfectly! I LOVED IT! It didn't need any alterations and it had to be one of the most beautiful gowns I had ever seen. It had a sweetheart neckline and huge, puffy '90's sleeves. I can still see in my mind's eye.

Here is where it becomes tricky when working with a coach. She didn't like it.

My coach felt that the color was too young for a Mrs. Pageant. I was only 26, but looked years younger and she was afraid that if I wore this gown, I would look more like a *Miss* than a *Mrs.* I could see her point, but I *really* wanted that gown.

We ended up finding a teal colored gown fully beaded that had dingle balls that fell from the shoulders and waist. What my friend Lisa and I called dingle balls were actually beaded fringe. Having never had a dog, we didn't realize that it was VERY close to a less desirable term and we definitely don't call them that (at least not in public) anymore! I *liked* the gown but didn't *love* it. It had to be altered and in the end it was fine, but sometimes you shouldn't settle for fine.

When the pageant weekend finally arrived, I honestly felt that I couldn't have done anything else to prepare. I was as ready as I would ever be.

I don't remember anything specific happening during rehearsals that was out of the ordinary. It was fun to see some pageant friends again from previous years. It felt great to be familiar with the process.

One thing that I remember about the interview was one of the questions.

"I see here that you are a Gemini. Geminis are known for having a split personality. How do you handle your split personality?"

WHAAAT??? That was definitely one question I had not prepared for! Here comes the weird part . . . the answer began pouring out of my mouth as if someone else was speaking the words for me! I remember sitting there thinking,

"This is GREAT! How am I coming up with this stuff?"

I can honestly say that someone from the great beyond was helping me in that room on that day and I thank them very much!

In case you're wondering, here is my answer (Yes, I still remember it!)

"Yes, (chuckle chuckle) I know that Geminis are known for having a split personality. If, however I feel my mood changing, I take a step back and breathe so that I don't ever portray the image of having a split personality."

(Or something like that, it HAS been 24 years!)

Preliminaries went great. Same with the pageant ball. Show up, mingle with the judges and off to bed!

The next day's rehearsal also went well. Nothing specific happened. Everyone practiced making the Top 10 and Top 5 just like the previous years, but now the nerves started kicking in.

Tonight was the night. I only had one place to go if I was going to move up at all. It is always a tough spot coming back as the previous year's first runner-up. The only thing you can do to improve is to win and the other contestants are well aware of that. Now . . . time for the show!

The opening number was great! It is always one of the most fun parts of the competition because there is no pressure. I don't know how I can put into words just how much fun it is to enter the stage and walk the runway to an upbeat, catchy, and fun song. It feels exhilarating!

After the *Parade of Beauty*, it was time for the Top 10 announcement. I was not called first. I was not called second.

Hmm . . . ??? Third . . . nope. Fourth . . . yes! That was me! Whew! I made it!

The onstage interview went well, thanks to the same great host as the previous year. Now time to change into swimsuit.

We were all given pink umbrellas to carry with us and they really did look very nice onstage. At least we ALL had to open an umbrella indoors! I remember one contestant REALLY did not want to carry it because her swimsuit was red, and it didn't match. We ALL had pink umbrellas. I'm sure the judges knew that she didn't purposely chose one that didn't match.

Sometimes you just need to let things go. Pick what you

chose to be upset about. Better yet, just go with the flow and don't be upset at all! Even though the judges can't hear what you say backstage, I always feel that it is best to put your best foot forward. Other contestants can hear you, as well as the pageant directors and chaperones. It's never a good idea to give yourself a bad reputation. Keep that in mind.

Evening gown went well also. No major hiccups. I remember one contestant had the most gorgeous white gown. It was fully beaded with long sleeves and a stunning scoop on the back. The winner from the previous year had worn the same gown in navy blue and it was even more fantastic in white. This girl was also very beautiful and very, very nice! She was going to give me a run for my money for sure!

Now it was time for the Top 5 announcement. For some reason I can't remember the order that the names were called, but I am pleased to say that I made it! So did the girl in the white dress. The husbands were once again brought up on stage for some fun and then it was time for the big announcement!

Fourth Runner-up . . . not me!

Third Runner-up . . . not me!

Second Runner-up . . . not me!

YIKES . . . it was down to me and the girl in the white dress! Aaaarrrggghhh . . . am I going to get First Runner-up two years in a row?

I CAN HARDLY STAND THE SUSPENSE!

First Runner-up is . . . THE GIRL IN THE WHITE DRESS!

I WON!

I could hardly believe it! All these years of hard work finally paid off. It was a feeling that is very hard to describe. It is always fun to win, of course, but winning after working so very, very hard is something completely different.

The rest of the evening was a whirlwind. Lots of photos, lots of congrats from family and friends, and lots of hugs from fellow contestants. I remember having breakfast in the hotel the next morning and still feeling dazed.

When my husband and I got home, there was a huge sign in the living room that read,

"Welcome home Mrs. Illinois!"

My husband had made and hung it up before he left for the pageant the day before. Nothing like positive thinking! (I'm not sure what he would have done if I had lost!)

The next few days were lots of fun. Celebratory dinners, phone calls and flowers seemed to be arriving at my house daily.

One thing that I remember CLEARLY was while I was driving one day, still a bit dazed, I sat at a stop sign waiting for it to turn green! I was thinking about the weekend and after a bit of time, one-by-one cars started to drive around me. I think it was about three or four cars that passed me before I realized I was just sitting there, staring straight ahead and not moving. I can only imagine what these people were thinking! I wasn't slumped over; I wasn't digging through my purse; I was just sitting there looking straight ahead! I am so lucky that one of those cars wasn't a cop!

The next few months were filled with appearances and hard work. One thing I learned after winning is that you have to line up most of your own appearances. The directors have certain events that their winners appear at every year, as well as some new ones, depending on the sponsors. For the most part, if you want to be busy promoting the pageant and any causes or charities that are near and dear to your heart, you need to work hard lining them up yourself.

My shift at the airport was 2:00 pm–10:30 pm, which meant that I didn't have to leave home until around 12:30 pm. I would spend just about every weekday morning making phone calls.

Some people were nice; some people were not.

Some people were confused and didn't know why I was calling them.

My best friend Lisa was a HUGE help through all of

this. For the events that I felt were odd for me to call myself, she would call on my behalf. One thing she had done was to call one of Chicago's big radio stations that had a booth at *The Taste of Chicago*. Without consulting me, she had lined me up to participate in their Velcro Jumping Contest! Yes, these people would put on a Velcro suit and run and jump off of a mini trampoline and fling themselves onto a Velcro wall!

WHAAAAT was she thinking?

I was not too keen on doing that but hey, it's all in good fun, so what the heck! Unfortunately, Chicago was hit with a very bad storm and the festival had to shut down early. I missed my one and only chance to go Velcro jumping!

One thing that happened around this time was my first taste into being a local personality. A friend of mine called me and told me to call this same radio station ASAP! They had received my picture previously, probably for the Velcro jumping event, and they were talking about me on the air. Apparently someone had called in saying that he went to high school with me and told them that I was "all over" the whole football team while in school. Seriously???

ANYONE who knew me in high school knew that that couldn't be further from the truth! The DJs were asking for anyone who knew me to call me and have me call them back. I did just that and since this man had also given his first name and said that he was a quarterback on the team, I promptly checked my yearbooks. Of course there was NO ONE listed by that name as a quarterback or even on the team at all. All was good with the interview . . . until one of the DJs said that he was taking my picture and going on a long bathroom break. REALLY? I was MRS. Illinois? Was that really necessary? Oh well, what are you going to do.

The next few months continued with lots of fun appearances. Parades were always fun and so were fashion shows. Again, I would find out why models are tall. None of the clothes fit me. Just about everything had to be pinned so that I wouldn't trip. I still loved and savored every moment, though since I knew I would never be able to be a fashion model.

One of the shows I was in, my best friend was able to come with and help dress me for each number. We had SO much fun! Having someone there to help you isn't necessary, but it sure does help. You really only have a few minutes to change between numbers. Fashion shows are very fast-paced, so it is quite helpful to have someone there helping. When it's your BFF, it's just that much better!

Another fun thing to do after winning a pageant is collecting your prizes! They had some amazing sponsors; I was very fortunate to win some fantastic things! My prizes ranged from a gas grill to luggage to clothing and the list goes on.

One prize that I really want to tell you about is from a very nice, upscale boutique that donated a suit for the winner. I was there with my directors trying on some amazing items and they were all very costly. I finally decided on a gorgeous, bejeweled sailor suit. (Anyone who knows me knows that I have an affinity for sailor clothing!) The suit was $400 and I felt guilty about getting it for free, but that was the price and, to be fair, everything in the store cost about the same.

This is where the story gets interesting . . . remember when I told you about my interview suit? The green, blue, and white suit that I had altered (and purchased for $39)? I said I would get back to it later. Well, now is that time.

One of the judges happened to be in the store that day. As we were standing at the counter wrapping up my item, Miss Teen Illinois walked in. The judge stopped to talk to her a bit and was explaining to her how important it was to have an amazing (as in costly) interview suit. She looked at me for reassurance and I didn't know what to do, so I just kind of nodded in agreement. She had NO IDEA when she was judging me that my suit cost $39 at Montgomery Ward's! MONTGOMERY WARD'S!

Those who may be a bit younger might not remember, but Ward's was a department store somewhat equal to Sears, but a few steps below in quality.

AMAZING! That just goes to show the power of a wonderful seamstress!

Something I really enjoyed doing was judging pageants. I really loved being on the other side and getting to know each contestant. Interview was especially fun since it was also a learning experience for me to see things from a judge's perspective.

One thing I remember clearly was when I was judging a teen pageant. This was back in the '90's when wearing a suit was protocol for an interview. One of the contestants came in wearing a formal cocktail dress. She looked very out of place compared to the rest of them, but I didn't want to mark her down without finding out why she made that choice. My first question to her was,

"Why did you choose to wear that dress today?"

I don't remember word-for-word what she said but she chose it because she liked it and it made her feel pretty. Her response convinced me to not mark her down and made me like her even more for making a bold choice!

Along with working some trade shows for sponsors I was also invited to attend a closing ceremony of the elementary school I attended when we first moved here from Sweden. The school was closing, and my teacher was still there and had contacted me to make an appearance. It was such a nice event! This is where I found out that I was the first non-English-speaking student at that school, something I did not know at the time. It was a beautiful and bittersweet ceremony and I was so thankful to see my teacher again!

One of the most fun events I was able to do was all thanks to my friends, Sue and Bruce in Peoria, IL. They arranged several days of fun things for us to do together. I remember going to Metamora and first meeting some of the locals. Then I was able to visit one of Abraham Lincoln's courtrooms. They even opened up just for me so that I could go in and take some pictures. They told me that the only other person they opened it for was President Nixon! Needless to say, they made me feel very welcome.

President Lincoln's Courtroom

We also toured the Peoria area where they had set up a radio interview and later brought me to a home for special needs adults. That was one of the most rewarding experiences of my life!

Once a month, they would have a dinner from a different country. Since I was Swedish, they went all out and cooked me quite the Swedish feast! It was amazing and so very thoughtful.

Later, some of the residents were proud to show me their rooms, which were very nice. Before I tell you the next part, I have to tell you about the outfit I wore. After I won, my trainer took me to her favorite boutique and bought me some fabulous outfits. One of them was a gorgeous green, silk blazer bedazzled with some various jewels and gold beads. It was very flashy and I loved it! I wore it with a gold top and gold stirrup pants. I was a '90's fashion plate for sure! I wore this outfit to my Peoria dinner. As I was walking back to the dining hall, I overheard one of the residents on the phone with her mom.

She was very excited to tell her that Mrs. Illinois was there and then I heard her add, " . . . but she has on the UGLIEST outfit I have ever seen!"

I just had to chuckle to myself and I really wanted to give her a hug, but I didn't want her to know that I heard.

After the Peoria festivities, it was time for the State Fair. I was there with some other queens and we did some fun things together. One of the events was a baby crawling contest. Each one of us had a baby at the starting line and their mom or dad was at the finish line trying to coax their baby to cross it first. Some parents used a toy, some used a set of keys, but honestly . . . most of them used a Remote Control! I would love to say that my baby won, and I really think it did, but I'm not sure.

Another event that I remember wasn't as much fun. It was the longest ponytail contest. We were in charge of measuring people's ponytails and how we did this was that we would place the end of the tape measure at the rubber band, put our hand around the ponytail and tape measure and slide it down so the tape measure was tight and then record the results at the end. I'm sure that reading about this doesn't make it sound too bad but let me tell you . . . it was cutthroat and DIRTY! First, if it wasn't bad enough that we got yelled at if the results weren't the same as the previous competition they were in, many of these people didn't wash their hair regularly and my hands were FULL of grease! UGH! *Let's change the subject, please!*

Another amazing appearance I had was meeting Marie Osmond. My director's daughter knew her personally and when she came to town to play a show, I was invited onto her tour bus to meet her. I remember having a HORRIBLE migraine that day, but there was NO way I was missing out on this! She turned out to be one of the nicest people I have ever met. I remember that when it came time for us to take a picture together, she ran to her bathroom to primp and touch up her lipstick. Marie Osmond had to primp . . . she's pretty much perfect! I felt like a hot mess that day with my migraine, but I still treasure that picture. Marie looks FANTASTIC and I look meh, but I still love it!

1992 was a very challenging year for me. Along with all the fun of being a title holder, I had quite a bit of stress in my life. My marriage was slowly falling apart from reasons not at all related to the pageant.

Photo by Dan DuVerney

I was also notified that I was selected into the Flight Attendant Training Program. After a time of soul searching, I made the decision that it wouldn't be fair for me to go to the Mrs. America Pageant and not have a secure marriage. I also knew that my First Runner-Up was very happily married (remember... she was the beautiful and kind lady in the white dress), and I wanted to give her as much time as possible to get ready for nationals. It was an absolutely heartbreaking decision, but I know it was the right one. My directors were very supportive and so was my First Runner-Up. She represented our state beautifully and I still continued to participate in the pageant for several years as a guest and a friend.

Now, off to (as we called it back then) Barbie Boot Camp aka . . . Flight Attendant Training.

CHAPTER 5

When Things Go Wrong—Take 1

SOMETIMES WHEN YOU COMPETE in a pageant, things go wrong. Not necessarily with anything you did, but human error takes place. To be fair, I will not name personal or pageant names because my intent is not to hurt anybody publicly but to inform you all that these things happen, and it is up to you on how you choose to handle them.

For my first example I will tell you about a certain *Ms.* pageant that I competed in. Since I was now divorced, I was no longer able to compete in a *Mrs.* pageant and *Ms.* pageants were now the category I fell into (yes, there are Miss pageants for young, single women, Mrs. pageants for married women, and Ms. pageants for everyone else). This one didn't have a huge contestant number, so they opted to have an *interview pageant* only. We all met at a certain

location in our interview suits and competed in a panel style interview and nothing else. It was actually very nice. Since there was no swimsuit or evening gown competition, my best friend Lisa decided to compete with me. She has always been heavily involved in helping me prepare so this was a fantastic opportunity for her to experience a true pageant interview.

I have to say that thanks to my training, interview is one area of competition that I feel strongly about. I tend to get high scores and I enjoy the whole experience. This one was no different. There was one girl there that we felt was our strongest competition. She was wearing a beautiful pink suit so I will refer to her as *Pinky*. When it was time to announce the runners-up and the winner, I was ready and hoping to at least make it into the top three.

2nd Runner-Up . . . Not me

1st Runner-Up . . . ME

Ok, so I didn't win. No biggie. We were sure that *Pinky* had it (and so did she as she took a step forward when she heard my name)! When they announced the winner, we were all a little surprised as it was NOT *Pinky*. It was a young girl who seemed very sweet but didn't seem to have too much pageant experience. I was happy for her.

I didn't think too much about it after that. You win some, you lose some. That's just part of the game. You just have to learn from each experience and prepare better in the areas that you fell short. I didn't know what went wrong, but I was about to find out.

It was either later that day or the next when I got a phone call from the Mrs. Illinois-America Director. She knew the director of this pageant and had received a phone call. The director had wanted to get a message back to me to help me prepare better for my next pageant. Her message to me was that I lost because I had said in the interview that in my free time I enjoyed driving around in my Mercedes convertible. Um . . . I don't have a Mercedes or a convertible and if I did, I would NEVER say that in an interview!

As it turns out, they had mine and the winner's scores mixed up! I didn't want to make a big deal out of it because this young girl was SO happy that she won, and I didn't want to take that away from her. Also, when a pageant result is disputed it can get very ugly. If it is a contestant disputing her own result, they will most likely look like the bad guy and a sore loser themselves. *More on that later.*

The national office called me and offered me the Ms. Minnesota title, but I didn't feel right representing a state I didn't have ANY connection to. I asked if Pennsylvania or New York were available since I had previously lived there, but they were not. They called SEVERAL times and lowered the entry fee to nationals each time, but I didn't feel right taking the title. In retrospect, I probably should have. I think the final offer was $450 for a 10 day pageant in Mexico!

WHY DID I SAY NO??? Oh yeah, ethics. No connection to Minnesota. Oh well. On to the next pageant!

CHAPTER 6
Ms. Illinois 1995

SINCE I WAS STILL SINGLE, I was not able to compete in a *Mrs.* pageant. When another *Ms. Illinois Pageant* came along, I jumped at the chance! There wasn't much shopping to do as I already had my competition wardrobe. The directors of the Mrs. Illinois-America Pageant were nice enough to let me keep some of my prizes when I gave up the title, so I wore a GORGEOUS Alyce gown that I had won, as well as my new favorite Sailor Suit. I wore the same swimsuit that I had previously borrowed from my trainer, so the only money spent would have been on shoes and accessories. It is possible to compete in a pageant on a budget!

The pageant was a lot of fun and I met some very nice women. I did, however have my first experience with a pageant *mean girl*. While I was *on deck* for the interview, which was a panel style (approximately 3 minutes with all 5 judges at the same time) one of the contestants came up to me and said, "I heard that they want you to spend the whole 3 minutes answering the first question they ask you."

REALLY??? *Obviously you think I'm competition since you think that rattling my nerves RIGHT before I go into interview would be a good idea. Do you really think I would fall for that???*

I just said, "Ok, well you go right ahead and do that."

That would not be the last I would hear from her!

The interview went smoothly as did the preliminary competition.

When the time came for the final competition, I was MISERABLE! I had a horrible migraine and could barely function. The pageant director also suffered from migraines, so we tried all sorts of combinations of over-the-counter medicine and caffeine. I was hurting all day but, as always, I REFUSED to let a migraine win!

On with the show!

The final competition went smoothly, until it was time to change into my evening gown. Remember that girl who tried to mess with me before interview? She was at it again! I had some boob pads tacked into my evening gown. Each one just had a little stitch on each side so that I could easily take them out after the pageant. My advice to you is to stitch them in properly and leave them in the dress!

She had twisted each one so many times that the lining was all messed up in the gown! You only have a few minutes to change between numbers and it took more than a couple of minutes to untwist the mess she had created. I prevailed and made it out on stage on time!

The rest of the pageant went without a hitch. I was called into the Top 10 (the mean girl wasn't!). I have to say, in my experience, the pageant mean girl usually doesn't win or place. Karma is a wonderful thing! The onstage interview went fine. Swimsuit and evening gown was fine. Now it was time for the Top 5.

I MADE IT! YAAAAAAAY!!

The Top 5 was an interesting group of women:
- Radio station promo model
- A young widow
- A psychologist who would later appear on *The Apprentice*
- A 40-year-old dentist
- And myself

So many different walks of life and they were all wonderful!

As the Runners-up were called, I realized just how lucky I was to be standing there. It came down to me and the dentist.

First Runner-Up . . . the DENTIST!

I WON!!

I was so very happy to have won, knowing that I would not have to give up my title for any reason and I was going to nationals!

I had many friends at the pageant and one of them went up to one of the judges and asked what she saw in me to make me win. She said it was my confidence on stage. **Keep that in mind**. You can be the tallest, thinnest and prettiest one there, but if you don't have confidence on stage, you don't have a chance!

Since I needed some new official headshots, I decided to go with a friend of mine. He was an aspiring photographer and was up for the challenge. We met at my best friend

Lisa's house and had a VERY primitive photo shoot. We hung a sheet up on the wall, took the lampshades off of two lamps. Lisa and the photographer's wife stood behind the lamps bending white poster board to reflect the light from the bare bulbs. We had a BLAST and the photos came out GREAT! Let this be a lesson, where there's a will, there's a way. If you absolutely can NOT afford professional photos (still the best option, though) you CAN have a good photo if you put some thought and effort into it. It's also WAY easier today with modern, digital technology and editing.

Photo by Dominic Messina

As the months went by, I heard less and less about the national pageant. I was so excited to finally get to go, but it was becoming more and more apparent that it wasn't going to happen. Then I got the dreaded phone call. The pageant had folded. BIG, BIG BUMMER!!

To be a first-time state title holder can be a wonderful thing, but it is also risky. A national pageant is very costly and sometimes directors bite off more than they can chew. Now I had this wonderful state title, but it would sadly end there.

CHAPTER 7
Mrs. Illinois-America 1997

BY 1997, I WAS REMARRIED, which made me eligible to compete in the Mrs. Illinois-America Pageant once again . . . if they would have me. I spoke to the directors about coming back and they in turn spoke to the national office. We wanted to make sure that everything was on the up and up since I had won five years before. The national office assured them that I was allowed to compete again since I had never been to Mrs. America. At that time, you were only allowed to compete at the national level one time. Because I gave up the title BEFORE I went to nationals, it was okay for me to compete again. I was assured that I would not have any preferential treatment, it was like starting over from scratch and I wouldn't have it any other way.

When you compete in a pageant, it is important to have the support of your family and friends along the way. I didn't have much of a support system in the beginning, but I built a great network of friends throughout the years. This time, though . . . for some reason it felt different. Maybe they saw that I wasn't quite ready to come back but didn't want to tell me? I wasn't overweight by any means, but I had had a baby the year before and hadn't quite lost all of the baby weight, but I still felt good. To be honest, I would be THRILLED to have that body today!

The preparations went ok. My trainer wasn't able to go with me to the designer to buy my gown, so I brought my mom. We tried on many gowns, but this time I couldn't find anything amazing. I bought one that was just ok. It was blue.

I found an interview suit that I liked, but my trainer didn't like it. I was able to get some new photos, but she didn't like those either. Having a pageant coach or trainer is great, but sometimes it feels a bit like *too many cooks in the kitchen.*

I had purchased an AMAZING emerald green and gold gown in a resale shop for $100 (ALWAYS check resale shops!) that I absolutely LOVED! When I went to my trainer for my final wardrobe decision-making, she still did NOT like my suit but ok'd it with some minor alterations. My swimsuit was fine (just fine . . . not great). My trainer adamantly wanted me to wear the blue gown for competition and the green one for the ball. I reluctantly did what she said.

Everything went fine over the pageant weekend, but nothing felt great. The interview was **fine.** I felt **fine** in my swimsuit and **fine** in my gown. What I think we've all learned so far is that **fine**, is not going to cut it!

I have to say that it was really tough and awkward to come back. Some of the other contestants knew who I was and knew that I had won before. It puts a target on your back to say the least. Nobody was mean to me, but I felt as though people were talking about me behind my back, and I'm sure they were.

When the top 10 were called, I luckily made the cut. The onstage interview was **fine** (again . . . **just fine**), as well as the rest of the competitions.

When it came time to call the Top 5, I didn't make it.

I saw my mom's face in the audience, and I will never forget it. She was EXTREMELY disappointed! I'm not sure if she was disappointed in the results or in me.

Needless to say, I was crushed! I would have been ok not winning if I had just made the Top 5, but not making that cut really hurt.

I don't want to put the blame on anyone but myself. Maybe I just wasn't ready to come back, but I really feel that if I would have worn the green gown, I would have felt more confident on stage and would have possibly made it.

Pageant trainers and coaches are invaluable, but if you don't agree, maybe you should move on to a third option until you are both satisfied. It is VERY important to feel put together, and when your coach doesn't agree on your decisions, you may start second guessing yourself and that is NOT going to cut it on stage!

I made a vow to myself that if I ever did this again, I would not let ANYTHING sway my confidence!

Sadly, this is the only photo from the 1997 pageant that I could find.

CHAPTER 8
When Things Go Wrong—Take 2

IN THIS WONDERFUL WORLD OF PAGEANTRY things can go wrong, as I mentioned in a previous chapter. Sometimes, however they can go HORRIBLY wrong and how you handle it will show quite a bit about your integrity.

Let me start by saying again that I in no way wish to hurt anyone so NO names or titles will be mentioned. You must also realize that these things do not happen very often AT ALL, but you do need to be aware of the fact that they sometimes do.

Several years ago, I had the good fortune of competing in a national pageant. I was very excited and prepared extremely hard for this event. I splurged and bought an AMAZING gown, a gorgeous new swimsuit, and a friend of mine lent me her SPECTACULAR wardrobe. To this day, I wish I still had that interview suit because it was fabulous! I was mentally and physically prepared and honestly felt that there was nothing more I could have done in advance. I WAS READY!

The location of this pageant was FANTASTIC! I had several friends with me, and I had more coming. It is always great to be out of state competing in a pageant and having

When Things Go Wrong—Take 2

a large cheering section. Having friends that work for the airlines doesn't hurt either.

The week leading up to the final event went without a flaw. We had great activities, wonderful outings and I met many amazing women. The judges were terrific, and I felt that my interview went as well as it could have.

As with any competition, you never know who will make it into the top 10. There are ALWAYS surprises, both in who makes it and who does not. This pageant was no different.

There were three women that my friends and I thought would be my biggest competition. We were also sure that one of them would be a *slam dunk* for making the Top 5. Surprisingly, she didn't even make the Top 10! When this happens, my friends and I have a saying (that we only say to each other and never EVER in public) and that is . . . "She must have said F&@K in the interview!" Obviously, she did NOT say that, but what we mean is that you never know how someone's private interview went. They may be the most physically beautiful woman there, but maybe their interview skills need some fine-tuning. The same goes for women you don't see coming. We call them *sleepers*. They are the women that may not be as put together as some of the others, but their interview skills are fantastic, so they make the cut. The best rule of thumb . . . don't worry about anyone else. Just be YOU!

I made the Top 10, as well as two women we thought would be tough to beat. The final competition went without a hitch except for one slight hiccup. Someone had the same swimsuit as me AND was right next to me! All you can do at that point is laugh and OWN IT! Do not ever let something like that get into your head. There will sometimes be women who have your gown as well. Some might even look better in it than you do. Oh well! Maybe your interview skills are better, and you have nothing to worry about. As a judge, I would NEVER let matching gowns interfere with my scoring, but your attitude will. Keep that in mind.

Now it was time for the crowning:

4th Runner-Up: Stiff competition woman #1
(I really thought she was going to place higher!)

3rd Runner-Up: Stiff competition woman #2
(WOW . . . yikes!)

2nd Runner-Up: A very sweet girl

1st Runner-Up: Me (Aaaarrrgghh . . . *SO CLOSE!*)

Now we REALLY didn't know who was going to win! The people we thought were my biggest competition had already been called out!

Winner: A sleeper we didn't see coming

Huh . . . you just never know, but now it got interesting!

I was proud of how high I placed and happy for the winner, but I was a little confused. Something didn't feel quite right. There was absolutely nothing wrong with the winner, she was a lovely woman, but something just felt off.

When I saw my friends after the show, it started to become clear. They had seen the owner of the pageant pick up the results from the tabulator, read them, crumple the paper and put it in his pocket, and gave the emcee a different sheet of paper.

When the winner was called, several of my friends looked at the judges and saw two of them look at each other and say, "But I had Illinois!"

As you can imagine, hearing this news was devastating to me, but it somehow made sense of the outcome. I really thought the 4th Runner-Up was going to win, and I would have been so proud to be standing next to her as the 1st Runner-Up. But to hear that it seemed the judges had picked me to win but the owner *fixed* the results, I was crushed. This was, after all, a national title.

I let myself be upset that night, but the next day I was mad and I wanted answers. I was able to track down the assistant director and she confirmed what we already knew. She said that yes, he had fixed the results because he had wanted this particular woman to win.

To keep things private, I won't disclose what the reasons were, but he thought he would not only have some financial gain, but also gain publicity by having her as the winner. The assistant director told me that I got off easy as he was horrible to work with and I was better off not being the winner. I was so confused and hurt. I had worked so incredibly hard and spent A LOT of money and I felt that it was all for nothing, as the winner was picked before we even got there.

I took the contract to a lawyer to see if it was worth pursuing anything, but I was told that the way it was written, I would have to fight it in the state where he lived and quite honestly, that sounded very costly. Now is where I feel integrity comes into play. I could fight these results in court, or I could just let it go.

Was I treated unfairly . . . yes. Did I deserve the title . . . if the judges' scores proved it, yes. Was I willing to tarnish my reputation in the process . . . NO! I had the common sense to know that if I fought this, there was a good chance that the media would make me look like a sore loser. I knew that I wanted to get to Mrs. America someday and fighting for the title of a pageant that is run by someone without morals is something that I didn't want to risk my reputation for. Keep these thoughts in mind as they will come up later in my story.

The reason I don't wish to reveal any names or titles is not to protect the unethical man who ran this pageant, but rather to protect the woman who won. To this day, I do not know if she had anything to do with what happened. If she was just an innocent participant, I don't want to take anything away from her.

Now it was time to take a little break, then dust off my heels, and do this all again!

CHAPTER 9
Mrs. Illinois-America 1999

WELL . . . HERE WE ARE AGAIN. Yes, I was DETERMINED to get to Mrs. America, so once again I was competing for the Illinois title. This time I had absolutely AMAZING support from my friends! Since not placing in the Top 5 two years before, I was going to make sure that there was nothing (and I mean NOTHING) I could have done differently to make me feel as prepared as I could be.

Since having a baby a few years before and being a little older, my body was different. Not necessarily bigger, just different. I wanted to make sure that I was in absolute, tip top shape. I wanted to be thin like I was before, but also toned and not just skinny. I went to a local weight loss chain and religiously ate their meals when I wasn't working. I ate VERY carefully when I was flying and worked out 2 hours a day (including 1,000 crunches daily). When I say daily, I meant it. There were times that I started my workout at 2 AM! WHAT WAS I THINKING??? I see now that it was a bit over the top and obsessive, but it worked. I had decided that since 13 was my lucky number, my weight goal was 113 lbs. On my final weigh in before the pageant, my weight was . . . 113! If that wasn't a sign, I don't know what is!

I went into this pageant a little differently this time. In the past I had always looked for ways to save money. This time I wanted the best (within reason, of course). I wanted to show a bold, not timid personality in interview, so I bought a red suit. My swimsuit is still one of my very favorites. It was green ombre and made me feel AMAZING! I spent more on my gown than I ever had. It was around $600, and I had some custom work added. I know that isn't a lot by some standards, but for me it certainly was. My best friend was there when I bought it and she said it was almost like she could see a halo around me when I put it on. That's how we knew it was "THE ONE"! It was a champagne color with copper beading. I had copper highlights added to my hair that really pulled out the colors of the dress and still went well with my swimsuit and interview suit. I WAS READY!

I booked a suite at the hotel so my friends Lisa, Jeanne, Terri, and I could all stay there together. (My husband came for the shows with our daughter but didn't stay at the hotel until the last night). We were a GREAT team! When I got up in the morning there were motivational signs taped everywhere in the hotel room. When I say everywhere, I

mean EVERYWHERE! Lisa had made them beforehand and there was even a sign printed in a mirror image so when she taped it to the wall in the bathroom, I could read it through the mirror! I still have all the signs and they mean the world to me!

We had quite a system for getting me ready. Everyone had a job. The best advice I could give you for staying organized is to have a clear garment bag for each outfit. I had the shoes laying on the bottom and a zip-lock bag hanging on the hook with all the accessories. This way nothing was lost, and everything was where you needed it. The garment bags were also labeled in order of events. After I got ready and went down to orientation my friends were getting my *Rehearsal 1* outfit ready for my very quick change before heading over the theater.

Orientation is always fun. Everyone is dressed in their 2nd best suit or dress (best is always saved for interview). Everyone is full of hope and excited to meet the competition and none of the claws have come out...yet. After sitting down and scanning the room, I saw instantly the two people who I thought would be my biggest competition! I will call them Comp1 and Comp2 (in no particular order). Comp1 was Top 10 with me in 1997 and Comp2 was Top 5 in 1998. We were treated to refreshments and listened with anticipation on what the next 2 days held in store. I felt more ready than I ever had, but also nervous as there was, as always some very stiff competition!

After orientation, I went back to our room for my quick change. Remember how I said everyone had a job? Here is where it came into play. While I was filling them in on orientation, one of my friends was in charge of changing my earrings (clip-on is always best for quick changes!), while another was in charge of changing my suit, while the third was changing my shoes. I had a totally new outfit on in probably less than 30 seconds! I had the best pit crew ever. Now, off to the theater for rehearsals.

My Pit Crew: Terri, Me, Lisa, and Jeanne!

This is the time where you may start to see things *happen*.

Sometimes you will run into that contestant (or contestants) who feel like playing mind games is the way to go. I have never fallen into that category, but I have competed with plenty of women who have. In this case, it started at rehearsal.

Rehearsals are always fun to me. It is the first time you get to walk the stage to that fantastic, upbeat song (this year it was BELIEVE by Cher and to this day it is still one of my favorites). The adrenaline rush is EXHILARATING! The opening number was still a state costume competition and there were LOTS of fun costumes representing Illinois! You again also use this time to introduce yourself as well as your costume to the judges and the audience. Now is when the first mind gamey thing came into play from Comp1. I understand wanting to stand out from your competition but there is a right way and a wrong way to do that. Comp1 decided to show off the fact that she could sing during her intro. Her costume had something to do with the Chicago theater scene and she decided to sing part of a musical theater song. As a pageant coach, I would NEVER advise my clients to do this! She had a lovely voice but in this case I feel that it was used to intimidate the other contestants. It gave me that same uncomfortable feeling that you get when you watch American Idol, and someone shows up to the audition in a bunny costume. It just isn't the right way to get attention.

When I told my friends they all said, "10 bucks she DOESN'T do that tonight when the judges are there!"

Guess what??? She DIDN'T! Just as we thought, she only did it in rehearsal in front of the contestants. Ladies . . . don't fall into this kind of thinking. It's ok to stand out (and you should), but there is a right way and a wrong way to do that. Intentionally trying to intimidate the other contestants is just not nice. I'm not saying this out of jealousy, I am a singer and musical theater performer as well. As far as pageants go, my singing is kept to the talent competition if there is one!

On a side note . . . in a recent Miss Universe Pageant, one of the semi-finalists decided to sing her answer during the onstage interview. She did not make the next cut.

After rehearsals, we were bussed back to the hotel for lunch and to get ready for interviews. This pageant will once again hold their interviews in a panel style: 5 judges on one side of a conference table and you on the other. It's a little intimidating but nice at the same time as your interview is over in literally 3 minutes or so vs. 5 minutes with each judge. I was very excited yet a bit nervous as this part is worth 50% of your score. Basically, if you blow it . . . you blow your chance of getting in the semi-finals! I knew in my heart of hearts that my red suit and I were READY!

Our holding area was by a door to the outside. People kept coming and going which made our area VERY VERY COLD! I started shivering and couldn't stop for anything. I was so afraid that the judges would take that as nerves which they weren't. I was just REALLY cold! Sitting there waiting you see A LOT of gorgeous women in AMAZING suits or dresses that probably cost more than your gown. It can be hard not to be intimidated. You just have to remember that they are not judging you on the cost of your suit/dress. As long as you look put together and wear something appropriate, you will be fine.

My interview came and went in what felt like 10 seconds. The only specific question I remember is that they asked me to sing them something in Swedish (I had on my bio that I can sing and act in 2 languages). I sang the Happy Birthday song and they seemed happy with that. The other questions were basically what I had prepared for and it was over quickly. Now I had a little bit of time to relax before prelims.

Prelims are always exciting. Standing in the wings waiting to go on is a feeling I will NEVER forget! When that music starts, and you head out in front of a live audience, your adrenaline will SKYROCKET! Just try to keep everything in check. The women who let the excitement take over will usually mess up their introduction. Do your best to try and stay calm, focused, and your intro will be flawless.

I really loved my costume this year. I was Sailor Jack from Cracker Jack. Some friends of mine at work made my huge Cracker Jack box and I wore my husband's Grandfather's original Navy uniform top from WW2. I was able to get some authentic WWII bottoms from the Army Navy Surplus Store and I felt honored to wear it. FYI . . . Cracker Jack made its debut at the Columbian Exposition (World's Fair) in Chicago in 1893.

The rest of prelims went great. Swimsuit and Evening Gown competition were fine. Again . . . I saw some amazing gowns but I really loved mine. I was really glad that I spent the extra money to have one that I truly felt great wearing.

During the rest of the pageant, another contestant started to stand out to me. We'll call her the *Sleeper*. Again, a sleeper is someone who you originally don't think will place very high but then, out of nowhere, ends up in the top five or wins. This woman was amazing, but didn't quite seem as prepared as me, Comp1, or Comp2. (I would notice later that her evening gown was too short. My guess is that she borrowed it, which is TOTALLY fine and a GREAT idea, just make sure it fits properly!) DEFINITELY some serious competition here!

After prelims, we went back to the hotel for the Pageant Ball. This is a fun event, but as always I didn't stay long. Just like before, they still want you to introduce your husband to the judges and mingle a little. We did just that and then I was off to bed! The contestants who stay the whole time really don't have their best interest in mind. You need to get as much sleep as possible and wake up refreshed, NOT hungover! You have a very busy and long day ahead and you want to be at your best.

The second mean girl moment once again came from Comp1. During rehearsals the next day, the judges came by for a short time to observe. Comp1 chose this EXACT moment to start passing out gift-wrapped cookies to the other contestants AND THE JUDGES! This may not sound like a big deal to you, but back then, we really didn't give out any kind of contestant gifts on the state level, at least not in this pageant. The judges were only there for about 30 minutes to see a small part of the rehearsal and passing out cookies to them was in my opinion poor taste. The judges were there to observe, not mingle, and by passing out a gift when no one else did, it made some of the girls feel as if they did something wrong by not bringing a gift of their own. Again . . . not a big deal, just a tiny little mind game.

That next day is spent at the theater rehearsing everything. Everyone practices making the semi-finals and the onstage interview. You also are taught how the runner's up, and winner will be called. I specifically remember them saying to make sure the winner faces the audience so that the photographer will get a great shot of her FACE and not her backside hugging the other contestants.

After rehearsals, we went back to the hotel to get ready for finals. The nerves were really kicking in now. This was the moment I had been working YEARS for and it was finally here! Since there was a smaller contestant number this year, they decided not to have any semi-finalists, and everyone would just compete again. They would pull the runner's up and the winner right out of the group. I personally don't like when pageants do it this way. I like when it comes down to the final two and they hold hands center stage waiting for that final announcement. It's so very suspenseful and exciting. I feel that pulling the winner out of the remaining finalists tends to lessen the excitement. I do, however understand why it is sometimes done this way, as it gives the First Runner-Up her moment in the spotlight. Just a personal preference, I guess.

Getting ready for finals was as stressful as usual. The hyper juices were kicking in. As I have said before . . . pageant diarrhea is a REAL thing! I once heard of a contestant having her hair done by her stylist while she was ON THE TOILET! If it happens to you . . . you are NOT alone!

The final competition went great and now it was time to announce the winner. I still felt strongly that Comp1 and Comp2 were my biggest competition, but I still had my eye on the Sleeper. She was such a lovely woman and could have easily taken the crown.

Here we go:

2nd Runner-Up: Comp2

1st Runner-Up (OMG, I'm so NERVOUS): Comp1

H@/Y CRAP!!!

Did I do this or did the Sleeper take it all? Was there someone else I wasn't expecting? SOOOO many questions and only one answer!

"Mrs. Illinois-America 1999 is . . . MONICA SKYLLING!!!"

OMG!!! I DID IT!!! I'M GOING TO MRS. AMERICA!!!

This was truly a moment that I will NEVER forget. All the years of hard work had finally paid off. All those 2AM workouts, strict diets, and interview prep . . . ALL PAID OFF!

My team and I were excited beyond words. And when I say team, I mean **TEAM**. I have the best friends anyone could ask for and we all did this together!

Remember when I said that we were told that whoever wins needs to face the camera after the crowning? Well . . . after my official walk as Mrs. Illinois-America 1999, Comp2 gave me a big hug, put her hands on my shoulders and promptly spun me around to face the cameras. She was SUCH a sweetheart! I will always remember that moment of good sportsmanship. Something others could learn from.

The rest of the night was a blur. LOTS of photos, collecting prizes, and chatting with so many of my friends that came to cheer me on. One funny thing sticks in my mind. I rode the hotel shuttle back to the hotel along with my director and I will never forget the words she said to me.

"Congratulations . . . you look beautiful . . . you need to gain 5 pounds!"

There you have it. There actually IS such a thing as being too skinny. So gain 5 pounds I did!

CHAPTER 10

When Things Go REALLY Wrong

THE NEXT FEW MONTHS WERE SPENT in total excitement at the prospect of FINALLY going to the Mrs. America Pageant! I don't even know if there is a word that exists that could possibly depict just how happy I was.

One morning while I was on a layover, my husband called me. He said he was listening to news radio and they started talking about me. He said that apparently I was being sued! HUH? For WHAT? Well . . . let me tell you. Remember when I said that Comp1 had been in the Top 10 with me in 1997? Well, she was bound and determined to get this title one way or another. She found herself a lawyer and went to the media, claiming that since I won this pageant in 1992, I wasn't eligible to win again in 1999. Hmmm . . . funny how it didn't bother her in 1997. Only when she stood to gain something by being 1st Runner-Up did it make a difference. If she had been 2nd Runner-Up, I really doubt anything would have come of it. Did she not realize that we went to the Mrs. America director in 1997 to make sure I was eligible to compete? Again . . . the ONLY stipulation in the contract was that you could only compete at Mrs. America once. I NEVER WENT! Also, since

I gave up the 1992 title, I was no longer recognized as the 1992 winner. Anyway . . . my world was about to be turned upside down!

By the time my husband came home from work, there were messages on the answering machine from Fox News, CBS News, WGN News, *The Chicago Sun Times* and *The Daily Herald*. When my flight landed in Chicago, I was afraid to go into the gate room. I had to send out my BFF, Jeanne, (who I was working this trip with) first to make sure that the coast was clear. By the time I came home, there were other messages from Judge Judy, Court TV, EXTRA and Inside Edition! This story hit the NATIONAL news in just a matter of hours!

This turned into a media FRENZY! To be clear . . . I was **not** the one being sued. She sued the pageant for allowing me to compete. In the days that followed, I was in newspapers all over the country. Seeing how a sore loser could turn this into NATIONAL news was very disheartening.

The media seems to latch on to anything pageant related and this story was about to get even bigger. Within a few weeks, Inside Edition came out to do a story. INSIDE EDITION! How in the world did this get so big? This was simply a case of bad behavior by a sore loser . . . and the media LOVED IT!

The next few weeks were some of the most stressful of my life. All of this took place while I was supposed to be getting ready for Mrs. America. Unfortunately, the lawsuit put a freeze on my prizes during this time, so I couldn't collect some of the things I needed such as headshots, gowns and other prizes. I ended up paying for some of these things on my own, which became very costly. The headshots alone were $1,000! My directors had to pay a lot of money for a good attorney who then instructed me to hire my own attorney who specialized in public cases. In other words, there was LOTS of $$$ for innocent people to pay! Luckily for me, my attorney, Vic Ciradelli, was not only very competent, but also very, VERY nice. His confidence and kind heart really helped to keep my nerves in check (as much as possible, anyway).

Why did I have to get my own attorney? Comp1's lawyers seemed to keep delaying things on purpose, trying to drag it on closer and closer to the Mrs. America Pageant. Since competing at Mrs. America was considered a *prize*, if they could keep delaying everything, eventually I wouldn't be able to go. That was their mindset . . . if Comp1 couldn't go, then I shouldn't go either! Can you see why I was stressed??? Also, we wanted to make sure that WHEN we won, she couldn't come after me personally with a separate lawsuit. My bases were covered.

During this time, very ugly rumors started to surface. One in particular was very hurtful. Someone spread the story that the reason I got divorced in 1992 was that I was sleeping with someone connected to the pageant. This couldn't have been further from the truth! The man in question is very nice and I had known him for years, but we had never even gone out for a cup of coffee, let alone a date. By this time, he was married to a WONDERFUL woman whom I adore, and this rumor was just mean and spiteful. I'm pretty sure I know who started this and we looked into suing for slander, but it would have cost us EVEN MORE

When Things Go REALLY Wrong

MONEY, so we decided to just let it go. We know the truth and that's all that matters.

After the Inside Edition story aired, it became more and more apparent that Comp1 was basically making a fool out of herself on national television. It looked more and more like a VERY costly case of sour grapes. At the end of the story they had a poll, "Should Mrs. Illinois keep her crown or should Comp1 take the title?" Needless to say . . . I won by a LANDSLIDE!

As the court date arrived, my nerves were at the highest level. As it turned out, I could have just stayed calm as the judge ruled in our favor almost instantly. Before we left the courtroom, my friend took my banner out of my bag and put it on me. I was escorted out by my lawyer to several news reporters waiting patiently with their microphones and cameras at the ready. It was a very odd feeling.

Some things I have learned:

- **Some newspapers will write whatever they want . . . even if it isn't true.** Among other things, a prominent Chicago paper wrote that I was wearing my banner DURING the hearing. I most certainly did NOT, as that would have been in poor taste.

- **The Associated Press can get your UNLISTED number in a heartbeat.** While I was on the train ride home from court just a few hours later, they called my unlisted cell phone for an interview regarding the hearing.

- **ANYTHING pageant related is BIG news!** The information on the lawsuit appeared on the COVER of the *Chicago Sun-Times* right next to a story on JFK Junior's plane disappearing. How could they POSSIBLY think this story was front page news?

The moral of this story is . . . DON'T be a sore loser! Comp1 might have come back and won it all the next year. After this behavior, she would have a REALLY hard time ever being accepted as a contestant in another pageant.

Just like I said in previous chapters . . . how you handle controversy in the pageant world says A LOT about your integrity.

Another thing to keep in mind, if you win a well-respected pageant title you will be in the public eye. As I have learned, rumors and bullying are not kept to high school students and are very prevalent in the pageant world. It is even tougher today with social media being what it is.

Just remember that rumors are just rumors . . . they are not true. The people that matter in your life will know the truth. When your name is out in the media and untrue things are said about you, defend them when you can, but always hold your head high and be proud of your accomplishments.

One thing is for sure, during this ordeal I had AMAZING support! Not just from my family and friends, but from my directors as well. The directors of the Mrs. Illinois-America pageant are a VERY tight-knit family and they treated me like one of their own. We ALL got through this together and I will be forever grateful for their kindness.

CHAPTER 11
Mrs. America

AFTER ALL THE CRAZINESS of the last few months, the time was finally here. I was going to MRS. AMERICA! This moment had literally been years in the making and I couldn't believe that it was actually happening.

How do I even begin to tell you about the magnitude of preparing for a pageant on this level? Let's start from the beginning . . .

After you win, your state title things move rather quickly. In most states, you win a lot of your competition items for nationals such as your evening gown, interview suit, and state costume (if there is a costume competition). You will usually have these items in plenty of time, but other things you will be responsible for on your own. Your needed wardrobe for one, will be MASSIVE! Some women are able to compete with a relatively small stash of clothing . . . I am not one of those women! My Mrs. America Pageant was spent in Honolulu, HI, for 2 WEEKS! When you have outings and rehearsals daily, that equals about 3 outfits per day including shoe changes. Here is how it looked for me:

3 outfits/day x 2 weeks = 16 CHECKED BAGS!!!

They funny thing is . . . I didn't win the unofficial

award for the most baggage! Someone had 21! Luckily I had perks/connections at work, which made it possible for me to not pay ANY excess baggage fees! I don't think I would be as lucky today, though, as most airlines charge for ALL checked baggage.

Where did I get all of this clothing? Well . . . let me tell you: I BORROWED THEM! The smartest thing you can do is borrow from your friends. Trust me, if they are pageant friends, you will be able to return the favor someday. When you are gone for so long and want to feel your very best at every event, it would be VERY costly to have new items for everything. This way I FELT like I had something new without the hefty price tag. Luckily for me, I had a friend with an AMAZING wardrobe who was the same size as me. I will forever remember her kindness!

Another item that is VERY important to have is an AMAZING headshot! Most pageants will have that as a prize but if they don't, you definitely want to invest in a good photographer and make-up artist. In my case, with the lawsuit I wasn't able to use the sponsored photographer, so I forked out the $1,000  bucks and went to the best-of-the-best at the time. This man and his make-up artist were simply phenomenal and anybody and EVERYBODY who were serious about winning went to them! They were on the road, so I booked a slot and my husband, and I flew out to New Jersey to shoot with them.

Sometimes photo studios are not what you expect them to be. I had seen their amazing work for years and I suppose I was expecting something kind of glamorous. This was NOT! Since they were on the road, they were set up in a hotel room (and not a very nice one at that). Needless to say, I was glad I was not there alone. . . until I met them. THEY WERE WONDERFUL! Such genuinely nice people!

I was there for a VERY long time and truly left feeling like I had spent the day with friends. Hair and make-up took about 4 hours. 4 HOURS! My lips alone took about 20 minutes. What was magical, though was that back then, headshots were black and white, so the make-up color combinations were not really something you would think to use for every day. I was fascinated.

The make-up artist taught me what to do and wrote down all the colors he used and what I should use at Mrs. America. That way, I could place an order with him and be prepared to do my own make-up at the pageant just like he taught me.

We became friends and I was later going to work with him and use his make-up on the women I was coaching. Sadly he passed away a few years later. I will always feel lucky to have spent that time with this amazing talent who I learned so much from.

Since I was their last client of the day, the make-up

artist left after he finished with me. The funny thing was, the photographer had his own palette and definitely knew what he was doing as well!

I was so nervous about getting a good shot. I had seen so many photos from this photographer and they were all amazing, but some of the people didn't look like their picture AT ALL! In pageantry, that is NOT a good thing. You don't want to walk into your interview and have the judges do a double take and not know who you are. I was worried for nothing. My pictures were worth every penny I spent on them and I will treasure them forever. Sadly, I can't refer any of you to this photographer as he passed away a few years later as well. It was so sad to lose such amazing talent so young!

Another thing that is very important and very, VERY time consuming is paperwork! I was sent a STACK of paperwork to be filled out. This would include your bio for the judges, info for them to read while you're on stage during the competition, and since this pageant was televised, there were also snippets for them to read while you were filmed on your outings. There were also release forms, medical forms, dietary needs . . . the list seemed endless and was a bit overwhelming, but I was GLAD to do it! *These forms are easier today with the help of modern computers, but when I first started competing all of this was done on a typewriter (and yes, I still have mine . . . just in case!).*

The judges bio is extremely important. This is something you may want to use a pageant coach to help with. At the very least, a second and or third (or fourth) set of eyes are needed to check for typos! I can't tell you how many times I have judged a pageant and have seen mistakes on the bio. One in particular that I remember is a contestant who had written that her favorite actor was Jack Tripper! She was a teen so I cut her some slack, but had she had one of her parents proofread it, I'm sure they would have caught her mistake and had her correct it to John Ritter. I'm sure she never made that mistake again.

FYI: Jack Tripper was John Ritter's character on the TV show, *Three's Company.*

Another thing not to ever, ever do is to hand write your bio. If you don't have a computer, use a friend's or go to the library. Nothing says *unprepared* more than a handwritten bio! More on bio's later.

Now it's time to pack . . . UGH! This should be fun, but it can actually be quite stressful. Just do your best to stay organized. Chances are you will be packing too much, but as long as you keep it organized you won't be overwhelmed. Having a checklist is imperative! I will include one in a later chapter.

Also, make sure that if possible, pack ALL of your competition items in your carry-on bag! You do NOT want anything getting lost. One thing you might not think of is to bring whatever kind of medicine you may need. You may get pageant diarrhea and you may not have time to wait to find someone with Imodium! You may also need allergy meds, migraine meds . . . you get the idea.

I was also at a pageant once when my arm broke out in hives. I needed some cortisone cream. One of the contestants had some but was VERY reluctant to give it to the chaperone to lend to me. I guess she wasn't interested in helping the competition. Not too many women are like this, but you never know.

It was a little surreal flying to Hawaii on my airline. My pageant coach (and friend) had also used her miles to upgrade me to First Class! There were 3 or 4 of us on the flight and we couldn't wait to get there! I took the opportunity to sleep as much as I could on the flight as I knew that once we got there, there wouldn't be much time for sleeping.

Here are some things my coach tried to prepare me for:

- Sleep when you can! If you take a long bus ride . . . take a nap.

- You will make friends while you are there, but you are not there TO make friends. Keep things in perspective.

- If people think you are competition, they may try to mess with your head. Take it as a compliment and move on.

- Take extra good care of your competition wardrobe and jewelry. THINGS GET DAMAGED AND STOLEN!

Once we arrived, we were treated like ROYALTY! After we collected our luggage, our bags were magically whisked off to the hotel while we were ushered to our assigned limousines. This is where the first of many mind-gamey things happened. I was talking to one of the other contestants (who was also very petite) about having trouble finding clothes that fit. Back then size 0 and 1 were not around. The smallest you could get in a suit was generally a size 4. Sometimes if you arrived at the store right after their shipment did, you could scoop up the only size 2 they received. We were talking about having trouble finding clothes that fit without altering them.

One of the taller women in the limo looked at me and said, "Just because you're a size 2 in one outfit doesn't make you a size 2!"

HUH??? She was closer to 6 feet tall and would have looked funny as a size 2 so I don't really know why she made this comment. She was also GORGEOUS! We were certainly not bragging about being small. We were just having a conversation. It was actually quite difficult being that little and finding clothes that were trendy in a small size. The "petite" stores generally only carried business or more matronly type clothes. Nothing you would wear at a pageant. I guess this is what my coach was talking about. I chalked it up as a compliment that she thought I was competitive. I suppose it was, as this would not be the last encounter I had with her.

When we arrived at the hotel, we checked in and went to our rooms to get settled. The Mrs. America Pageant staff did an amazing job assigning us to our roommates. It was nice to see that they took the time to read our information and paired us up to someone they thought would be a good fit. My roommate ended up being another Flight Attendant for my airline.

That night at the orientation dinner, the national director made me cry. All he said was: "Welcome to the Mrs. America Pageant," and I was in tears! SO many years of hard work and I was actually there (in Hawaii no less)! I just couldn't believe that I was lucky enough to be one of the women sitting in that room. I'll never forget the feeling I had that night as we stood outside watching the fireworks over Waikiki and thinking of how incredibly blessed I was!

The next 2 weeks were filled with amazing moments. I could write a whole book on that experience alone (maybe I will someday), but to keep it brief, we were treated like celebrities the whole time we were there. Everything was top notch. We had amazing activities planned almost daily from lunch at the governor's mansion, filming at the waterpark, horseback riding on the beach, tour of the Dole Pineapple Plantation, tour of the U.S.S. Missouri, a submarine ride, Germaine's Luau . . . I could go on and on, but you get the idea. Along with all these activities we also had rehearsals. We were VERY busy to say the least! Now I know why my coach told me to nap when I could.

At a national pageant of this length, you have to pace yourself. If you don't, you will fade quickly. You will notice that the people that are SUPER outgoing in the beginning will be fairly quiet by the end. They are burned out. If you are there for the Congeniality award and not the crown, that's one thing; otherwise be nice to everyone but remember you are there for a (possibly 2-week long) job interview! You need to be strong the whole time. If your pageant is shorter, say less than 1 week, it may not be as much of an issue. Just be aware.

One funny story that I remember is that one evening we were having dinner with a prominent figure in the hotel chain where we were staying. It was a beautiful formal event and we all were wearing full length gowns. When they started serving food, we ate our salad (and maybe soup, I don't remember) then they brought out this amazing coconut shrimp. We all (at my table) assumed this was the main course and since we hadn't been eating too much the previous week (upcoming swimsuit competition) we were STARVING! Needless to say . . . we started devouring this shrimp! The server actually had to come up to us and say, "You ladies might want to pace yourselves . . . you still have 4 more courses coming!"

I really wish a camera had captured the look on our faces. It must have been PRICELESS!

As we got closer and closer to the final competition, it was also time for our families to arrive. I'll never forget that day. My husband, daughter, mom, and aunt were due to arrive at around the same time that I was to be out on a submarine ride. I remember starting to walk from the dock and got to a spot where the sidewalk split. I stood there thinking how they could be just about anywhere since this resort was so large. I just stood there and waited for a *feeling*. I definitely got one and went the direction my feeling told me to go. Lo and behold who comes walking toward me but my mom and my aunt! It was very cool!

As far as some mean-girly things that happened during the week, for one, that girl from the limo came up to me and asked me who was in my Top 5. I told her I wasn't sure since there were so many strong competitors. She didn't hesitate to tell me hers, in which I was not included. I suppose that meant that I really WAS in her Top 5!

Also, something that happened to me several times was that someone would ask me a question and while I was answering would walk away. Was this some kind of weird mind game to make you think what you had to say was unimportant? I never had this happen before and since several women did it, I had to wonder if it was a *thing*. It was very odd!

When we received our swimsuits, they were very large. Just about everyone had to have them tailored. As luck would have it, my aunt is an amazing seamstress and she took care of mine with no problem. One of the ladies had her suit stolen and swapped for an ever larger size! Since so many women had to have theirs altered, the tailors at the hotel were swamped! One of the contestants asked me what I had done with mine. I told her my aunt fixed it for me and she asked if my aunt would fix hers, too? I really didn't know what to say.

She then said, "Oh . . . why would she . . . I'm the competition!"

It was weird . . . even I hated to ask my aunt to fix mine as they were BUSY! They had some serious sightseeing to do. They were in HAWAII!

By now, rehearsals were in full swing. I always enjoyed rehearsals. I loved the upbeat music and the dance numbers and this one was no different. I have to say that this opening number routine was rather difficult. I really felt bad for the ladies who didn't have any dance experience as they were struggling. As it turned out, during the telecast, several women ran into each other on the stage while we were supposed to alternately cross over each other. OOPSIES! Since it was taped, the TV folks were able to splice the routine together to look ok on TV. I really wish I could see the original recording of the whole number. It was so much fun to do!

Before we knew it, it was time for the interview competition. YIKES! Always scary . . . always fun! This pageant would be different for me. I was used to the panel style interview (where the judges are all sitting on one side of a conference table and you on the other). This one you had one-on-one time with each judge. It was AMAZING!

When you are preparing for a pageant interview, you have general answers prepared such as your favorite movie, favorite book etc. My answer for my favorite passenger was Florence Henderson. She was on one of my flights with horrible weather delays and to make matters worse, when we finally arrived, the jet bridge was frozen in ice! All in all, she and many other people were on my plane for SEVERAL hours more than they were supposed to be, and they were NOT happy.

Florence however did not say a word. She never complained and kept her sweet disposition the entire time. I even got a hug as she was leaving. When I got to the interview I realized that her daughter was a judge! WHAT WOULD I SAY IF SHE ASKED ME WHO MY FAVORITE PASSENGER WAS? If I said it was her mom, she would think I was lying! Luckily for me she didn't ask, and she was as nice as her mom.

One judge was an artist and I felt like we hit it off talking about all of my arts and crafts. As I was leaving another judge, my banner pin caught the chair, dragging and tipping it over.

The only thing I could think to say was, "Well, THAT was graceful." And she laughed.

All in all, everyone was nice, and it was the easiest interview I had ever had. I just had to wait until finals night to find out if they actually liked me.

Now it was finally time for the preliminary competition. While we were backstage getting ready, I saw something I had never seen before: a long line of topless women waiting for their turn with the chaperone. Huh? I really had no idea what was going on. I had to find out! Turns out they were waiting to have their boobs duct-taped together! A chaperone stood there with the tape and scissors, the ladies would bend over holding their boobs and would literally have them taped together. OUCH! That had to be fun to get that off later! It did give you great cleavage, though. Hmm . . . you learn something new every day.

Getting ready for the evening gown competition was really fun. Up until then, you hadn't seen anyone's gown and they were amazing! One was prettier than the next. Again, at this point you just have to remember . . . there will always be women there with gowns that are more expensive and prettier than yours, but they are not YOU!

The only thing I remember from the prelims is that while I was on stage, the judges didn't really look at me too much. They spent much of the time writing notes. I really didn't know if that was a good thing or not. I also remember my 3 year old daughter rushing the stage. ALL she talked about since I had won my state title was walking on the stage and talking in a microphone at Mrs. America. Her dad had to hold her back because she was determined to get up there!

At some point during the last week, they started building the stage for the final competition. It was going to be held outside with the ocean in the background at sunset! The rehearsals were really intense as they were held outside as well. It was VERY hot! We all wore sunscreen and a lot of us had to buy hats. We were also afraid of getting tan lines that would interfere with our gowns.

If I could give you one bit of advice to take with you forever it would be this: WEAR COMFY SHOES WHENEVER YOU CAN! You don't have to wear six-inch heels during your outings. SAVE YOUR FEET! My blisters were so bad I felt like I had to perform major surgery in my room every night just to try and relieve some of the pain. I heard that women from previous years had to go to the emergency room because their blisters got infected. Yes, I was limping on stage during the finals. You can see it in the telecast. It was AWFUL!

Before I knew it, finals day was here. We were all stressed, tired, and EXCITED! Just like previous pageants, we had to practice making it into the Top 10, then the Top 5. I was in the pretend Top 5 when they were calling out the pretend runners-up. Usually they will not call out anyone as the pretend winner or they will make one of the staff the winner. That was not the case here. The producers made me the pretend winner. Ugh . . . I'm not gonna lie . . . it made me feel a little jinxed.

I remember the previous year's winner whispering to me during the pretend crowning, "I begged them not to do that."

Oh well, nothing to do about it now.

Since the show was taped, the final competition took about 4 hours. The feeling of being on that stage with the TV cameras and Hawaiian dancers is something I can't put into words! It was one of the most exhilarating moments of my life! After the opening number, we came back out in our state costumes and then again in our swimsuits for the announcement of the special awards and the top 10. The moment of truth. It was scary, but at the same time not. There was literally nothing else I could do. Either I was going to make it, or I wasn't.

The moment was here:

Semifinalist number one is: MRS. COLORADO

Semifinalist number two is: MRS. ILLINOIS

OMG . . . I MADE IT! I made it into the Top 10 at Mrs. America! I will truly never forget that moment!

After the Top 10 were announced, it was rush rush backstage.

First, we had to come back out for swimsuit competition (you can REALLY see me limping in this one)! Then we had to go backstage to change into our evening gowns.

Here comes another moment I will never forget. They had a separate room for the non-finalists where they had food and a place to just relax during the competition until they were needed on stage again for the crowning. When I got back to the dressing room, one of the non-finalists was standing there holding my evening gown ready to help me into it. I am actually tearing up writing this as that is one of the kindest things anyone has ever done for me at a pageant! She said that the ugly talk was so bad in that other room that she didn't want to be in there. Apparently people were less than happy that some of the women made the cut and they did not. This happens at EVERY pageant! You never know what happens in the interview.

After the evening gown competition, it was time for the announcement of the Top 5. Quite honestly, I was THRILLED to make the Top 10 and didn't know what to expect for the rest of the night. Here goes:

First finalist	MRS. ALABAMA
Second finalist	MRS. MASSACHUSETTS
Third finalist	MRS. TEXAS
Fourth finalist	MRS. UTAH

At this point, I looked out into the audience and saw my mom. She looked SO NERVOUS! I gave her a look saying, *"It's alright . . . I made the Top 10 AND I get to be on the telecast . . . I'm ok."*

And our Fifth and final finalist is . . . MRS. ILLINOIS! O . . . M . . . G . . . I MADE THE TOP 5 AT MRS. AMERICA!!!

At this point, I was truly in shock! The happiness that I felt at that moment is something that I will never forget. To think that all those years of hard work, all those 2-hour workouts at all hours of the day and night would culminate in a Top 5 finish at Mrs. America was truly remarkable.

At this point, we had a Top 5 interview. Honestly, I could have done better but that's ok.

When it came time to announce the final outcome, I was called out as the 4th Runner-Up. As fate would have it, the winner went on to become Mrs. World and the First Runner-Up took over as Mrs. America. By this happening, we were all *bumped up* a notch and I can now proudly say that I am 3rd Runner-Up to Mrs. America 1999!

Not too shabby if I do say so myself.

CHAPTER 12
Coaching

THE NEXT SEVERAL YEARS WERE SPENT raising my kids (shortly after the Mrs. America Pageant, I had my son) and working as both a Flight Attendant and actress/model. I was blessed to be able to perform in several musicals, as well as becoming a graduate of the famed Second City, Chicago! I had the honor of performing on the same stage that so many Saturday Night Live cast members got their start. I can still remember the first time I stepped out on that stage. It was like I could feel John Belushi's presence and positive energy in the room. He was somehow there supporting all of our dreams and it felt amazing.

During this time, I also signed with a major talent agency in Chicago. This really kept me on my toes commuting into the city for various auditions and I loved it!

I was also able to stay involved in the pageant community as a coach, judge, and coordinator. I still loved everything about pageantry, but coaching held a special place in my heart. Ever since I can remember, I have always loved teaching. I remember teaching my friends how to knit, crochet, and later how to apply make-up. In retrospect, I probably should have become a teacher, but somehow my career path didn't lead me in that direction.

I loved taking the information that I had learned in all my years of competition and passing it on to other women. For those of you who seek out a pageant coach, just remember . . . they do not have an *in* with the judges. It is also up to you to take what you learned and put it into action. I'm not saying that you  have to do EVERYTHING your coach tells you to do, but you have to remember that they have experience and you are paying them to share that with you.

After several years of coaching, I worked with a couple of women that made me wonder what they really wanted to achieve through coaching. Whenever I worked with a new client, the first question I always asked them was, "Why are you competing?"

That may sound like a weird question, but it really isn't. Some women, especially in a *Mrs.* Pageant have always wanted to compete at Miss America or Miss USA, but for whatever reason were never able to do so. This is their chance to live out a lifelong dream.

For them, coaching may just be a way to make them feel more comfortable on stage. They may not have any big desire to win, they just want the experience. There is absolutely NOTHING wrong with competing for this reason! I find it admirable to put yourself out there, most likely WAY out of your comfort zone to live out a dream. I love coaching these women! There is no pressure, just a lot of fun.

Most women, however, are *in it to win it* and that is a whole other ballgame. We spend several weeks together, working on all levels of competition. I'll cover more detailed info on coaching and preparation in a later chapter but trust me when I say we work on everything, I mean EVERYTHING!

Here are some examples:

- Your reason for competing
- The Interview
- Your Judges Bio
- Physical Fitness
- Headshots
- Ad page
- Evening gown
- Wardrobe
- Stage Presence
- On-Stage Interview
- Make-Up
- Hair

There are of course other things more individualized for each person. Some need more work in certain areas. Some do not. Some women have many years of experience; others are just beginning their pageant journey. One thing is for sure, I always make my clients sign a statement stating that coaching does NOT guarantee you a spot in the Top 10. Unfortunately, some women do not seem to understand that statement.

I have coached many women. Some win, some place, and some do not. There is an odd phenomenon that I noticed with a few women that made me ultimately take a break from coaching for many years.

As I said earlier, you do NOT have to listen to EVERY word your coach tells you. The ultimate decision is up to you. You do, however have to live with the outcome.

After coaching for several weeks, some women, after learning quite a bit, will start to feel like they know more about pageants than I do. I quite honestly felt like they were paying me to tell them how great they were. That may sound harsh, but that is how I felt. They began to argue if I made a suggestion and would refuse to listen to my advice. One woman in particular ended up doing the exact OPPOSITE of what I suggested! I ended up telling her that I didn't think our coaching time together was a good fit and that it seemed she wanted to do this on her own. Coaching isn't for everybody and that's fine. She begged me to keep her as a client and I reluctantly did. She continued to do everything opposite of what I suggested or more specifically what I highly recommended she NOT do. Needless to say, she did not make the Top 10 (even though she was extraordinarily beautiful). She called me at ONE O'CLOCK IN THE MORNING crying and wondering why she didn't place!

That is when I hung up my coaching hat for many years.

CHAPTER 13
Competing in the Latter Years

AFTER TAKING MANY YEARS OFF from pageants, I figured that I was basically retired. Then one day, my husband said to me, "I think you should compete in another pageant."

He was actually serious, and my response was, "I'm almost 50!"

His answer was simple . . . "So?"

He was right. So what? So what that I was almost 50? Is it so bad for a 50 year old to want to be in shape AND do work in her community?

Now it got interesting.

There are three main pageant systems for married women: Mrs. America, Mrs. United States and Mrs. International. Since I had already competed at Mrs. America, I wanted to experience something new. I have had many friends involved with the Mrs. Illinois-International Pageant and I also knew that the directors were absolutely WONDERFUL, so to say that I would be proud to be a part of this sisterhood would be an understatement.

After submitting my application, I was accepted as a

contestant and had a few months to prepare for the state pageant. There was no turning back now.

When I first started competing in "Mrs." Pageant, I was in my 20s. I was naturally thin. I didn't have to work out and I had to work hard to keep weight *on*.

When I was in my 30s, I had to THINK about working out and I would lose 5 pounds. I did, however train hard for the Mrs. America Pageant because I wanted to be toned and not just thin.

My 40s consisted of working out and watching what I ate and struggling quite a bit with weight fluctuations.

My 50s . . . UGH!

I had to get up every day at 5:00 AM and work out in my home gym for an hour and watch absolutely everything I ate. I went to a local weight loss support group and had some success but never got really toned. When pageant time came, I was at a pretty good size but nowhere near what I had been when I was younger. After having my daughter when I was 31, my body didn't really change that much. The only significant difference was that my bustline went from a 32A to a 34B. Once my son came along at age 36, MANY things changed! My bustline shot up to a 36D and I actually got hips! None of this was a bad thing at all. It was kind of fun to finally have some curves! I just had to REALLY work out so I wouldn't get TOO curvy.

I didn't seek out a coach, which in retrospect I should have done. As in all things, changes had taken place in the years since I had last competed. For example, I was determined to find the PERFECT interview suit. I had shopped for MONTHS to find one. What I didn't realize was that interview suits at pageants were pretty much outdated. Women now wore dresses. That would have been MUCH easier to find! Since make-up trends had also changed, I was only a little prepared for this and clearly not as much as I should have been.

I did seek help from a few friends, but I really feel that I should have paid for some one-on-one time with a coach involved with this system. Being that this was a platform based pageant, as well as having fitness wear instead of swimsuit competition, it was different than what I was used to in previous pageants.

Pageant weekend was a BLAST! I met some amazing women who I am still in touch with today and the directors and former winners did a wonderful job putting on a fabulous affair.

All areas of my competition went pretty well . . . except for one.

The onstage interview.

I bombed. I bombed BAD!

We had to give a prepared statement on our platform (mine was Domestic Violence Awareness). Easy enough. I'm an actress. I can recite a script or monologue without any difficulties, at least you would think.

This was literally less than 30 seconds . . . of HELL!

For some reason, I couldn't remember the first word of my speech. Here is my thought process: LAST YEAR'S WINNER:

"Tell us about your platform."

ME: "Uhhhh . . . ."

OMG . . . what is the first word?

I can't believe this is happening to ME!
This happens to other people, NOT a trained actress!
   ME: "Uhhhhh . . ."
What do I do?
People are staring at me.
I have to say SOMETHING!
   ME: "Domestic Violence is really bad."
What did I just say?
Did I just say that Domestic Violence is REALLY BAD?
DUH!
OF COURSE IT'S REALLY BAD!
OMG . . . I'M GONNA END UP ON YOUTUBE!

After that, the rest of my speech came out ok, but it really threw me off my game.

Needless to say . . . I didn't place. I did win the photogenic award, of which I was very proud, since there was only one for all age groups. I have it proudly displayed in my trophy case today.

This was not the end of the road for me, though . . . it just fueled a fire.

The next year, I was awarded the title of Mrs. Illinois-United States 2016 and I was headed for the Mrs. United States Pageant. I was VERY excited since this was one of the other *Big Three* pageants for married women. I could not have asked for more support from my family and I had about 8 months to prepare.

This time I wanted to do everything I possibly could to feel prepared. First things first . . . I hired a personal trainer. My workouts became almost obsessive. I worked out 5 days a week, 3 hours a day, including 2 sessions a week with the trainer. This went on for months, until I went to nationals.

I also continued going to the weight-loss support group I had gone to earlier, but I couldn't seem to get past a certain weight no matter what I tried. I came to the realization that they promoted eating quite a bit of processed food. Once I switched to non-processed and organic food, I broke the plateau. I left for nationals at a weight I was happy with. I wasn't as toned as I would have liked, but I felt good.

I also shopped 'til I dropped for just perfect outfits for EVERY event! My flight benefits also brought me out to Los Angeles and the LA Fashion District to buy my gown. (I HIGHLY recommend doing this if you have the means!) It also put me in touch with a terrific hair and make-up artist who also coached me and has since become a wonderful friend.

FYI . . . even coaches can benefit from working with a coach when they compete. It is ALWAYS beneficial to have another set of eyes!

When I arrived at nationals, I felt that there was nothing else I could have done better to prepare. I was blessed with the best roommate anyone could ask for (who was a little younger than me, but we were both not 20 somethings) and we were ready for the time of our lives!

Being that this pageant was only 5 days long, it really

wasn't fair of me to compare it to the 2 weeks I spent in Hawaii competing for Mrs. America, but it was hard not to. Instead of having outings out on the town (in LAS VEGAS) promoting the pageant, most of our days were spent either in rehearsals or having free time. Although the free time was nice, I would rather have had more time getting to know the other contestants.

They did, however have some AMAZING parties in the evenings. The first night was spent at a pajama party. We all got to meet each other dressed in our favorite PJs which was a HOOT! I found a really fun sleepy shirt that I thought was *perfect* for a pageant (It says: *"NO PHOTOS PLEASE"* in **SEQUINS**!). Other ladies were dressed in everything from flannel PJs to a fuzzy elephant. It was especially fun since they had Miss Congeniality playing in the background.

Another party they had was a very elegant *White Party*. I had never been to one before, but it basically just meant that everyone had to dress in anything they liked as long as it was all white. I have to say that this was STUNNING! Scanning the room and seeing this sea of pure white was truly beautiful. That night was also spent doing the traditional contestant gift exchange. This is always such a fun event. I brought each lady a Chicago Cubs' mug filled with food and candy that originated in Illinois. I came home with so many fun and meaningful items from the other contestants that I will always treasure. (To this day I still use some of the items I received at Mrs. America 1999).

If you ever have to do a gift exchange, just remember . . . you have to transport your gifts to the national pageant. Make sure your items aren't too heavy and are easy to pack. One of the gifts I remember receiving that I truly loved was a photo of the contestant's state flower along with a description of her state. This is something that I could easily put in my scrapbook to remember her by and it didn't take up ANY space in her suitcase. BRILLIANT!

My favorite party was the Costume Showcase. It was an evening spent with all of us presenting our costumes for the first time by walking a runway that was set up to resemble New York Fashion Week. It was the first time our families would see us in action, and it was relaxed, fun and something I will always remember.

When it was time for the private interview, I was ready. I had found my favorite dress of all time and I felt amazing in it. I truly felt that this was one of the best interviews I had ever had. One judge was difficult, but she was difficult with everyone. I feel that she just wanted to see how we all handled the really tough questions and I felt like I handled it well. She seemed very satisfied with my answer, which made me feel good.

As the days moved forward, I was more and more thankful for my roommate. I started to feel like I was in high school as the cliques were definitely forming. I think this happens at most pageants, but I had been lucky enough to not have experienced it before. Needless to say, older *mom* types of women were not welcome in these cliques. Had it not been for my roommate, I would have felt rather alone. I am the type of person who can easily make friends with just about anyone (something I have to do at my job every day) and although this wasn't true of everyone as I met some truly nice and amazing women, it made me a little sad to see how many grown women would just ignore me when I tried to get to know them.

When it came time for the preliminary competition, I was excited to get the show on the road. My best friends Lisa and Jeanne had arrived (as well as my mother-in-law) and we were ready! (When I say we, I mean WE. Lisa and Jeanne have been a part of my pageant journey since almost day one and that will NEVER change.) I love being on stage and this pageant was no different. I had worked EXTREMELY hard with the help of my trainer and I couldn't wait to get out there!

To be 51 years old and go out onstage in a swimsuit and compete against women in their 20s was exhilarating. I was so proud of the work I had done, and I think it showed. I had never felt better about my body because I had worked so hard this time. I felt like I looked better physically than I had in my 20s or 30s and I'm sure that showed in my confidence.

I absolutely loved my gown and my state costume is my very, very favorite of all the costumes I ever wore. Lisa and I made and bedazzled it together and we are very proud of it! We have made many costumes over the years, but this one was special. This costume represented the Chicago Cubs, who would later go on to win the World Series that year for the first time in 108 years!

I felt very satisfied with my performance in the preliminary competition and didn't feel that I could have done any better. When the final competition was in full swing and it came time for the announcement of the Top 15, I didn't know what to expect. This pageant was known for choosing women who were basically bikini models and that was not me. I felt really good about my performance but no matter what I did, I was not a bikini model. There are always surprises and this pageant was no different. One by one women were called out and one by one they were not me. As it turned out, this would be the first pageant I competed in that I did not make the cut. I was a little sad, but I was by far NOT devastated!

My roommate and I broke out the chips and chocolate backstage and pigged out! I was actually more upset about one of the other contestants not making it. One of the girls there was EVERYTHING that this pageant is known to look for. She is beautiful, kind, smart AND is a bikini model! I messaged her after it was over and told her that I was more upset about her not making the cut than me. As it turned out, she went back the next year and won the whole thing! Yes, I'm a big dork and cried happy tears when I heard the news and she ended up being an AMAZING Mrs. United States!

Now that I had competed at two of the *Big Three*, I had one left. To compete at all three of these pageants representing the same state would make you a *Triple Crown Holder*. It is an *unofficial* title but cool nonetheless. Since I won Mrs. Illinois-America twice, this would actually make me a *Quadruple Crown Holder* and the only one in my state to say that. I decided to follow this path and I would now be heading out to compete at the Mrs. International Pageant the next summer.

As always, I had the amazing support of my family and friends, but I wasn't quite feeling it at the gym. I worked out but not as hard as I had the year before. This pageant didn't have a swimsuit competition but rather fitness wear. My personal preference is for swimsuit, but I completely understand why some women prefer fitness wear. I suppose I just prefer wearing heels onstage as they make my legs look leaner than sneakers.

I had amazing support from my directors (whom I absolutely adore) and we had a lot of fun getting me ready. The only difference I found with this pageant system was that I didn't have as much freedom of choice. My official headshot was chosen for me and it was not one I would have picked myself. In all the pageants I had competed in previously, I had ALWAYS chosen my own headshot so this made me very uncomfortable. The photos are always your first impression with the judges, and I felt that my first impression could have been much better. The photographer was great, I just wish I would have been given the opportunity so see all the shots before one was chosen for me. My gown also had to be registered months before the pageant. This bothered me quite a bit as well, as I still had weight to lose and I really didn't want to select my gown that early. The reason for this was so that no two people had the same gown. Quite frankly, it never bothered me if someone had the same gown as I did. You are two different women; the gown would look different on everybody but that wasn't the case here.

Another issue before the pageant, was that they changed one of the areas of competition. Up until then, the onstage interview was that platform statement that I had bombed onstage two years before. I signed up for this pageant knowing that this time would be different because I would be more prepared. Now, however I found out that they changed the onstage interview for the finalists, and it would be a current event type of question. By now, I had already signed a contract and it was too late to back out.

In all my years of competition, I have usually steered away from pageants that ask these types of questions. I prefer pageants that want to know more about the person as an individual and what they can bring to the title through their community service, not their opinion on the gross national debt of Latvia!

It's not that I am unable to answer these types of questions, I just choose not to put that kind of pressure on myself. It's one thing to be prepared for the *possibility* of being asked a current event question and another thing ENTIRELY to KNOW you will be asked one!

Anyway . . . I was stuck. I had to move forward.

When I arrived at the pageant, I was pleasantly surprised at how organized it was. The hotel was amazing, and the directors seemed very nice and professional. Another nice surprise was that the food was phenomenal! I have a lot of food allergies and this pageant did an AMAZING job to make sure I didn't go hungry. I had meal prepped beforehand and brought a weeks' worth of food with me just in case and I definitely didn't need to eat any of it. The staff and especially the photographers were fantastic as well.

This week was off to a GREAT start!

The week was spent with several outings and events. The rehearsals were also made to be extra fun because of the very nice and professional choreographers. It's so important for the reputation of a pageant to hire kind people to be on their staff and this pageant was topnotch.

I once again had a wonderful roommate, but boy did I *click* with one of the other contestants! We were inseparable! She truly made this one of the best weeks ever and I will never forget her!

I also had another amazing connection with a different contestant. While people will tell you that pageants are a sisterhood, I can honestly say that families click as well, and many times stay connected for years to come.

The private interview and preliminary competition went well. I felt good about all of it. I was however REALLY nervous about the onstage questions for the finalists. As it turned out, I didn't have to worry as I once again did not make the cut. Sitting in the audience watching the interviews, I can honestly say that I have never been so happy NOT to make the finals! The questions were horribly difficult and not weighted evenly AT ALL! I felt so  bad for the women who were up there and had to make heads or tails out of these questions that I actually started tearing up for them. The winner was amazing, and I was very proud of her. In fact, all of the finalists handled themselves very well during this difficult phase of competition (even though I could see the struggle on some of their faces).

This is just another example of being sure to do your research *before* entering a pageant. There are MANY systems out there and each one focuses on different things. Some pageants are big on the political or current event questions, whereas other pageants don't even allow those types of questions to be asked at all. Some pageants are platform based, whereas some are not. It is up to you to choose what type of pageant suits you and your personality and go from there. There is no right or wrong pageant, just what is best for you.

Sadly for me, I found out about this change AFTER I signed the contract. I still had an amazing time and I am SO proud to be Mrs. Illinois-International 2017.

CHAPTER 14
Not All Pageants Are Alike

NOW THAT I HAD COMPETED for many years in many different pageants, let me start by saying that most of them have been amazing and positive experiences. There are, however a few negative things that I have come across along the way that I would like to share with you. Some things I want to mention as helpful tips, while others are to remind you of the importance of doing your research beforehand. Also, if you are a pageant director yourself, some of these things should definitely be placed in the *DO NOT DO* column of your checklist.

One pageant that I was in did not schedule ANY meals for the contestants. NOT ONE! Eating together as a group is such a wonderful time to get to know one another and this pageant never gave us the opportunity to do that. If you can't afford to feed your contestants at the hotel, maybe you could check how much it would cost to have boxed lunches or salads delivered to the rehearsals. Anything would be better than not getting to eat together at all. If your pageant has a high entry fee for the contestants, it would seem very odd to not at least put some of that money towards feeding them.

Another time I had an issue with the hair and make-up

artist backstage. At the time I had some acne and she asked that I stop by to see her before heading out onstage in my swimsuit so she could give me a touch-up. I remember asking if she was SURE I had enough time and she assured me that I did. Well, not only did I NOT have enough time, I had to walk out onstage while EVERYONE was already out there! I was mortified to say the least and I'm sure the judges picked up on my late arrival. I suppose that I assumed that she would have communicated with the person running the show to hold up for a moment. Sadly, she did not, and all this did was make me look even worse than if I had just gone out with my acne in full view.

It is also very important to have a proper and well-lit changing area for the contestants. You will usually find these to be an actual dressing room if you are at a theater, or possibly a conference or banquet room if you are at a hotel. Most important, it has to have good lighting and mirrors. I had a very odd experience once where the dressing room was in a closed off bar area. Needless to say, it was VERY dark! There was virtually no lighting and they only had a few dorm room type full length mirrors leaned up against the wall a little here and there. We basically couldn't see anything. Sadly, the area I was set up in didn't even have any chairs or anything for us to sit on. It was also up several flights of stairs. There was an elevator, but it was known for getting stuck. Could you imagine getting stuck in the elevator during the show? You wouldn't make it out on stage in time and I REALLY didn't want THAT to happen again.

To be safe, I chose to take the stairs which was a fun thing to try and do in six inch heels and a gown that weighs

500 pounds (not really, but you get the idea)! They also didn't have anyone backstage (at least not where my dressing area was) to help you get dressed. This was definitely a first for me. Every pageant I had competed in ALWAYS had someone there to help you. Not only was the room extremely dark, but everyone around me was already backstage when I was trying to change into my gown. Because there were no chairs, I opted to keep my shoes on when stepping into my gown since it would have been too difficult to sit on the floor to put them back on with my big fluffy gown. My heel got caught in the lining and I went down headfirst into the floor. My knee was clearly injured . . . BADLY! It was banged up and scraped and I was just lying there on the floor in a pretty decent amount of pain. If that wasn't bad enough, I heard several women behind me (who clearly had to have seen me fall) passing me by . . . one by one . . . without a care in the world that someone was hurt. I had to roll over onto my back and ask one of them to help me up. This woman actually made a *face* at the fact that she had to be inconvenienced in such a way! Can you believe it?

The next day I went to the staff and told them what happened. I asked if they could at the very least have chairs set up for us for the final competition so no one else would get hurt. Not only were there no chairs set up for us during finals, no one even seemed to care that I had been injured.

This was certainly disheartening, especially because I could compare it to another time when I had an instance where someone could have been hurt. During the rehearsals, my heel got caught in a crack on the stage. No biggie, these things happen. The choreographers saw it and

INSTANTLY asked if I was ok. I was TOTALLY fine. Just to make sure it didn't happen again, they stopped rehearsals and had someone come up and tape up the crack so that no one would get hurt. This is how it is done! You see a problem and you fix it. It's as simple as that. You definitely don't ignore a contestant who was injured, ESPECIALLY when you can see just how bad the injury was.

Speaking of choreographers . . . pick someone who is good at what they do, organized and NICE. They will get NOWHERE with your contestants if they are mean. I was in a pageant once where the choreographer was so condescending and mean that she had me in tears on several occasions. She seemed very unorganized in her teaching method and many of us were very confused. I certainly didn't want to ask any questions, though, as she had yelled and publicly humiliated SEVERAL contestants and I did NOT want to be the next! I just sucked it up, positioned myself towards the back of the group and hoped for the best. As a director, this is NOT a good way to get contestants to recommend your pageant for the following year!

All of these experiences, both good and bad have helped mold me into the person I am today. Another thing that you have to remember is that directors change. You could enter the exact same pageants as me and your experience could be totally different (both good and bad).

I definitely don't feel like my competition days are over. I just need to find the right pageant for me at this stage of my life. For now I may just focus on coaching and my career (both flying and acting). One thing is for sure . . .
YOU HAVEN'T SEEN THE LAST OF ME!

PART II.

GETTING READY

As I said earlier, the reason *why* you want to compete will help determine the type of training and preparation you will need. Another important factor is the type of pageant you wish to be a part of. If you only take one thing away from reading this book it is this:

Choose Your System Wisely!

Since pageant systems can be so different, one person's strength is another person's weakness. You may do well in one pageant system but not so well in another.

   Here is an example:

- If you have a very strong platform and or are very busy volunteering in your community—you may want to choose a platform based pageant.

- If you're in great physical shape and hope to further your modeling career—you may want to choose a more traditional beauty pageant.

- If you have an amazing onstage talent—find a pageant with a talent competition.

- If you have great communication skills—find a pageant with a 50% interview score.

- If you don't feel comfortable in a swimsuit—find a pageant with fitness wear or no physical fitness category at all.

As you can see, there are many pageants available and they all specialize in different things. Do your research ahead of time and you will find the pageant that is perfect just for you.

Don't feel bad if you feel stronger in certain areas of competition. Everyone does. You just have to find the pageant best suited for you and do your best to be prepared for ALL phases of the competition. That's where finding a good coach will be very beneficial. Just make sure you stick to ONE coach only. If you work with more than one, you may get some conflicting advice which could make you confused and unsure of yourself.

Find someone you trust, have a good connection with and there will be no limits to what you can accomplish.

If you can't afford a coach, that's ok, just be sure to read books such as this one and study up. There are also helpful tips all over the internet. You just want to make sure that the information you find is from a reputable source.

The next few sections will focus on each phase of competition. Make sure you read, study and take notes. Before you know it, you'll be in tip-top competition shape!

PAPERWORK

The first most important thing you need to do to begin is to send in your application. Most pageants today will have the application available online. In case they don't, just make sure you do NOT fill out a paper application by hand! That just SCREAMS that you are unprepared! Just scan it in, fill out each section on your computer and print the completed document. There are several programs available to help you do this.

Next is the judges bio. Same rule applies here. This MUST be neatly typed and printed. This is the form that the judges will have during your private interview. You definitely don't want their first impression of you to be, *"Oooohhh . . . she is sloppy!"*

This bio will have several questions about YOU. It is very important that you do not put what you think the judges want to hear, but rather what is true about who you are as an individual. When answering these questions, a good rule of thumb to remember is the *Rule of Three.*

What this means is to answer the questions in three parts. Some coaches will recommend that you put as much information as what will fit on the lines. I see the point that they are trying to make . . . to give the judges as much information as possible, but I look at it a bit differently. As a judge, you have a LOT of bios to read through before the pageant and if you don't get them until the actual interview, you don't have time to read everything on there.

Here is an example:

HOBBIES: Singing, acting, and ALL arts and craft work.

or

HOBBIES: Singing (karaoke and musical theater), acting in musicals and plays, as well as film work, knitting, crocheting, needlepoint, macramé, scrapbooking, jewelry making, and sewing.

What looks more professional to you? As a judge, I would have time to read the first one and be able to ask questions on the type of singing or the type of arts and craft work which is a great intro to your interview.

The second one . . . honestly, the judges may not have time to do more than skim it. In doing so, they might not retain much information. I would rather give them a few key points that I know they will remember, rather than risk giving them so much that they don't remember anything at all.

You also want to make sure that the information you give them makes you stand out from the other contestants. The types of questions you will normally see are:

Hobbies: _____

_____

Interests: _____

_____

Special Talents: _____

_____

PAPERWORK

_____

_____

Most recent community involvement: _____

_____

_____

_____

School: _____

Occupation: _____

What is unique about you: _____

_____

Why do you want to be Miss/Mrs._____?

_____

_____

What would winning the title mean to you? _____

_____

Something interesting about you: _____

_____

What would you do with the title? _____

_____

This is just a sampling of the types of questions that are usually on the application and bio. Again, you want to make yourself stand out. Give the judges information that sets you apart from the other contestants. It may even ask that exact question.

Let's use that as an example:

What sets you apart from the other contestants? _____

_____

Just remember . . . everyone is:

Passionate about their platform . . . approachable . . . hard working . . . etc.

Instead, tell them something like:

Languages you speak, extensive travel, or perhaps a unique career path. I have competed with 2 women who were either currently working or studying to be a **Funeral Director/Mortician** . . .

Now THAT'S unique!

Here's another one:

HOBBIES AND INTERESTS: I love to read, cook, and play soccer with my siblings.

This is a great, short and sweet answer. I'm sure the judges would have time to read the whole thing, but let's see how we can make it more interesting:

HOBBIES AND INTERESTS: I love to read, cook, and play soccer with my 10 brothers and sisters!

By giving the judges that little bit extra, you just punched up your answer, made the judges take notice, and gave them a GREAT question idea (someone would DEFINITELY ask about your large family) AND you made yourself stand out from the other contestants!

You're still not taking up too much space, but you're giving that little extra to your answer with something original (and of course whatever you list MUST be true)!

Maybe you have a fascinating hobby:

HOBBIES AND INTERESTS: I love to read, watch movies, and play my Didgeridoo. (You would probably be asked about the Didgeridoo!)

or

HOBBIES AND INTERESTS: Skiing, playing tennis, and teaching the ancient art of Origami at my local park district. (You would probably be asked about the Origami!)

These answers are short and sweet but still have something interesting *and original.*

(FYI . . . I'm just giving you ideas to think about. These are not necessarily true about me. I'm just giving examples to make a point. You have to find something that is TRUE and ORIGINAL to you!)

Again . . . remember the *Rule of Three*. If an answer can be answered in three parts, do it in three parts! Anything less and your answer will be too short, anything more and your answer will be too long.

Something very VERY important to remember is to have more than one person proofread your paperwork! You can read it over and over and miss the same typo every single time. One person might catch one thing, while another will catch something else. Remember that girl who put Jack Tripper as her favorite actor? Had she had it proofread by her parents, they would have caught this error FOR SURE and she would have put John Ritter! Details matter.

INTERVIEW

THE SINGLE BEST ADVICE I CAN give you for your interview is . . . KNOW YOUR BIO! The worst possible thing that can happen is that a judge asks you to elaborate on something you wrote down and you can't remember what that was. It makes you look like a liar.

Now, as far as interviews go, there are usually two kinds . . . **panel** or **one-on-one**. Here are some general guidelines for each:

Panel

In a panel style interview, the judges (usually 5) will be sitting on one side of a conference table with you on the other. When you walk in, make sure you are smiling BEFORE the door opens so they don't see the terrified look on your face before you start to smile. That will make your smile look fake. As you walk in and approach your chair, smile and make eye contact with all the judges as you say hello, feel for the chair with the back of your legs and quietly take a seat.

INTERVIEW

Do NOT cross your legs! If your skirt is short. . . they will see the whole show. You can either rest your feet on the floor or you can cross your ankles. If you chose to cross your ankles, be careful when you get up. You don't want your feet to get tangled up because of nerves and end up with your face planted firmly into the carpet!

Some pageants will have you make a brief statement at this point. This is your time to SHINE! The judges will know if you are to make a statement and they will give you a moment to begin. They won't say . . . *"Ok, Monica . . . you may begin."*

If you don't start talking, they will think you are not prepared, and they will just start asking you questions. You just lost an amazing opportunity to tell them about yourself.

If you are to make a statement, here are some guidelines:

- Do NOT tell them things that are already on your bio; they already know them. Tell them something that isn't on there and makes you stand out!

- Keep your statement to about 20 seconds or so. You don't want to lose time when they could be asking you questions.

- Make eye contact with each judge while you are talking.

- Make sure to smile (if appropriate).

- Make sure you have 3 distinct parts (*Rule of Three*). It could be something unique about you, what you have done to prepare, and what you plan on doing with the title.

Back to the part about not telling them anything that's on your bio. This is where many women flub a little. As a judge, what would make you sit up and take notice:

- "Hi. . . . my name is Monica, I have been married for six years and I have two children . . ."

or

- "Preparing for this pageant has been an amazing experience for not just myself, but for my entire family . . . "

Which statement would make you want to learn MORE?

I would want to know how your family was involved. Judges already know your name, age, children, occupation etc. . . . all these things are already on the bio you gave them. Tell them something interesting, something you want them to know about you that will make them ask questions.

Remember . . . not all pageants will have you make a statement (you'll know this in advance). The judges may go right into asking you questions.

The first question could very well be, "Tell us something about yourself that you want us to know."

It is best to be prepared!

In a panel style interview, you want to answer the questions in a particular way (as always, don't forget the Rule of Three). You will begin your answer by making direct eye contact with the judge that asked it. You will then look at each of the other judges, making eye contact with them as well and then finish your answer with the asking judge, again making eye contact. It is very important to include the whole panel for every question. They all obviously didn't ask each question, but they will all hear your answer, so you want to make them ALL feel included.

It is also acceptable to use your hands, but not too much. You don't want your hand gestures to take away from what you are saying. And as always . . . remember to SMILE when you talk (when appropriate). This is something you can practice at home in a mirror before the big day. If you don't smile, you run the risk of looking nervous. Just make sure you are not smiling while talking about a somber subject (homelessness, domestic violence, drug abuse etc. . . .).

When the bell goes off and your interview ends, finish your thought, quietly stand up and thank the judges for the interview. They will be thanking you as well. As you get to the door, turn around and give a big smile as you say, "Thanks again" or something similar. The reason? The goal is to ensure that your smile is the last thing they will remember seeing of you and not your backside!

One-On-One Interview

WAAAAY EASIER!

Panel interviews are usually 3–5 minutes and are over in the blink of an eye. That part is good. One-on-one's are usually 3–5 minutes with **EACH JUDGE**! That part can be a bit intimidating because your overall interview will last about 30 minutes. Don't let that bother you. It will still be over in the blink of an eye.

The one-on-one style interviews that I have done had me enter the room with 4 other women (one per judge).

You will go up to one of the judges and stand with your back to them until they say, "You may begin." That is your cue to turn around, introduce yourself, and have a seat. You will LITERALLY just have a conversation with them. They will ask you questions, you will answer, and you both will basically just chat.

As far as answering your questions, just remember:

- Make eye contact
- Smile when appropriate
- Use your hands as necessary
- Rule of Three
- And most important, BE YOURSELF!

Remember, this is a JOB INTERVIEW. You need to BE PREPARED! You wouldn't go into a job interview without researching the company. This is no different. Do your research about the pageant. Why did you choose this pageant over another one? If you get the program in advance, research the judges. (This only happened to me once. You usually won't know who they are until you walk in.)

If this is a platform based pageant, KNOW YOUR PLATFORM! I can't possibly express how important that is. You need to have facts, statistics, and whatever relative information you can get your hands on. You need to be able to answer questions about your platform intelligently. You will need to tell them what you have done with your platform in the past and leading up to this pageant.

Most important, you will need to tell them what you plan to do (in detail) with this pageant title to help further your work with your platform in your community, state, or country (or even world). If you can't speak freely and intelligently about your platform, it will look like you just chose something for the pageant. The judges WILL pick up on this and your chance of winning will be GREATLY diminished!

The most important thing is that you be yourself. The judges will notice if you're just saying things to impress them. If you don't usually use big fancy words in your daily vocabulary, don't use them in the interview. You will come across as fake, Fake, FAKE!

Another thing to keep in mind is that the judges are just regular people, even if they are a celebrity. They are probably a little nervous as well.

Something else to think about is that unlike the panel style interview, this time, only one judge will hear your answer. If you answer something well, only one judge will hear you; if you TOTALLY mess up . . . only one judge will hear you.

One time when I was judging a one-on-one style interview at a teen pageant, one of the contestants sitting in front of me was in the middle of answering a question. She must have chuckled or something because all of a sudden, a GINORMOUS SNOT-BUBBLE blew out of her nose!

YES . . . IT DID!

H@/Y CRAP!!

WHAT DO I DO???

She was as shocked as I was! I just pretended to be taking notes, trying to make it look like I hadn't noticed, and this girl was a ROCKSTAR! She could have EASILY run out of the room in tears (especially being so young), but she kept going as if nothing had happened and you know what... NONE of the other judges knew anything about it because it was one-on-one!

In case you're wondering about her score, I gave her extra points for how she handled it. Bad things happening aren't going to ruin your chances of winning the title, but how you handle them might. It is VERY important to remember that. I have seen several pageants where the one contestant who fell flat on her A$$ on stage left with that crown on her head because she handled it like a pro.

When the bell goes off, you finish your thought, stand up, and thank the judge for the interview. You will move to the next judge and stand with your back to them just like before and wait for them to say, "You may begin."

Everybody will have a preference as to what type of interview you like better, but just remember, whichever one you get... YOU CAN DO IT!

The best thing you can do is be prepared. Here are 100 questions to get you started. Some questions are ones that I feel are extremely important to be prepared to talk about (not verbatim, just an idea of what you want to say) and some questions are included to just get your mind thinking.

Interview Questions

1. Why do you want to be Miss/Mrs. _____?
2. What would you bring to the title of Miss/Mrs. _____?
3. What sets you apart from the other contestants?
4. Why should we choose you to be Miss/Mrs. _____?
5. What is your greatest accomplishment?
6. What is your favorite book?
7. What is your favorite song?
8. What is your favorite movie?
9. Who is your favorite actor?
10. Who is your favorite actress?
11. Who is your favorite singer?
12. Who is your favorite author?
13. What is the greatest thing facing your country today?
14. Are today's teenagers too into their looks?
15. What is the greatest thing affecting teens today?
16. Would you prefer to work for a man or a woman?
17. Tell me about your platform.
18. What is the very first thing you would do with the title if you win?

19. Give me three words you would use to describe yourself.
20. If you could do one day over again, what would it be?
21. What woman past or present do you most admire?
22. If you could have dinner with one celebrity, who would it be and what would you ask them?
23. What is happiness to you?
24. What is your greatest strength and what is your greatest weakness?
25. Besides your family and friends, what is the one thing you could not live without?
26. What would you say to someone who thinks pageants are sexist and objectify women?
27. Community service is very important, tell me about the last community service project that you were involved in.
28. What is the most important word in your vocabulary?
29. Do you have a special message to give to women?
30. If you felt a law was unjust, what steps would you take to change it?
31. Do you feel that violence in movies, television, and video games cause violent behavior?
32. If there is an obstacle in your way when obtaining a goal, how do you remove it?

33. There is much discussion on the media influence in the political process, what is your opinion on this?
34. If you could live your life as someone else, who would you be?
35. If you could change one thing that has happened in your life, what would that be?
36. If you were a judge, who would you vote for and why?
37. What have you learned about yourself from competing in this pageant?
38. If you could be a fictional film or literary character, who would you be?
39. Who or what makes you laugh?
40. If you could know one thing about your future, what would that be?
41. Tell me your most embarrassing moment.
42. In your opinion, what makes a woman truly beautiful?
43. What is your favorite color?
44. Why did you choose that outfit for today's interview?
45. What makes you angry?
46. What do you look for in a friend?
47. What would your best friend tell us about you?
48. What are you most proud of?

49. What motivates you and why?
50. What is your worst habit?
51. What do you expect to get out of this pageant?
52. Why are you competing?
53. What is your most unforgettable family experience?
54. What makes you sad?
55. What have you done to prepare for this pageant?
56. Where do you see yourself 10 years from now?
57. What is the best advice you have ever received?
58. What is the best advice you would give?
59. Who is the person that has most inspired you in your life and why?
60. What is your definition of integrity?
61. Do you think higher education is important today? Why or why not?
62. How would you like to be remembered?
63. Why do you want to win?
64. How do you plan on managing your time as a titleholder?
65. Why did you choose this pageant?
66. What do you like most about this pageant system?

67. What is your dream?
68. If you could go back in history, who would you meet and what would you ask them?
69. What is the most valuable lesson in competing in a pageant?
70. What are your thoughts on the swimsuit/fitness portion of the competition?
71. What is your opinion on the LGBT community?
72. What is the first thing you are going to eat after this pageant?
73. If you could travel anywhere in the world, where would you go and why?
74. If you had to choose a different platform, what would it be?
75. Describe what it means to be a winner.
76. Do you feel that education in the arts should be increased?
77. What would you do if you found out a friend or a family member was involved in an illegal activity?
78. Some people have cosmetic surgery to change their appearance. Would you, why or why not?
79. Have your values been influenced by what you watch on TV?

80. If you were to be stranded on an island, what one thing would you have with you?
81. Would you rather be a snowflake or a rainbow and why?
82. Do you think a woman is unfulfilled if she doesn't have children?
83. What is your mission in life?
84. If you found out that one of the other contestants had received the final questions in advance, what would you do?
85. What is the most important decision you have had to make?
86. Tell me a joke.
87. If I gave you a dollar, what would you do with it?
88. There is a fine line between self-confidence and conceit. How would you explain the difference?
89. What is the most interesting thing about you?
90. Do you believe in fate?
91. How do you relax?
92. Give me a 15 second commercial on your hometown.
93. What is your favorite phase of competition?
94. What is one thing you would change about yourself?
95. What is the biggest mistake you have ever made?

96. What would you do to prevent cyber bullying?

97. What is your perfect day?

98. What is one thing you have learned about yourself from competing in this pageant?

99. What is one thing you would like the judges to know about you?

100. What is your passion?

Bonus U.S. Only Questions:

- Who is the Vice-President of the United States?

- Who is your State Governor?

- More people vote for American Idol than the President. How would you change that?

- If I asked you to sing the National Anthem, would you know the words?

- What does being an American mean to you?

- Did you vote in the most recent election?

- What kind of car do you drive? (If it's not American, be prepared to tell them why.)

- How would you encourage people to buy more American made products?

- Do you think the Electoral College needs to change?

- How would you improve the quality of education in the United States?

Your pageant may specify that political questions are not to be asked. That does not mean a judge won't ask them. Be ready for anything. Also be ready to talk about all current events, especially the ones pertaining to your region. Watch national news, sign up for news alerts on your phone, do whatever you can to be aware and form an opinion on what is happening around you. The more time you spend preparing, the less of a chance you'll have of getting stumped.

I recently witnessed a contestant who was asked onstage about a VERY current issue in Europe. She had NO idea what it was! It was heartbreaking to see her stumble through her answer. Do your very best so this doesn't happen you. If you have a news-aholic friend, have them quiz you every few days on current issues. Any help you can get will help you to feel prepared.

As far as the voting issue in the United States, if you are over 18 REGISTER TO VOTE! If you are asked something about voting (Who did you vote for . . . How would you encourage more young people to register to vote, etc. . . .?) NOTHING you say will mean anything if you aren't registered yourself. If you are not registered, be prepared to give a VERY good reason as to why not.

What you wear for the interview will make an impact as soon as you walk in the door. You want them to take notice. Wear whatever color makes you look and feel amazing. You can wear a dress, suit, pantsuit, jumpsuit . . . pretty much anything goes these days, just so it's appropriate. You don't want anything too low cut or a skirt that is too short. It is, after all a job interview.

One thing in particular that I tell my clients is that

unless you have a very bold and strong personality, stay away from red. You may want something a little softer to match your sweet disposition. Also make sure your jewelry isn't too distracting. You want them to be focused on YOU. The bottom line is . . . make them remember you. Even if the scores don't carryover after the first cut, they will still remember an amazing interview.

Now . . . let's talk about the dreaded onstage question. It's really not that much different except A LOT more people will hear your answer. Still, the same things apply (rule of three, eye contact, smiling . . .). When you are brought up to the microphone, stand in a comfortable stance with your arms at your side. Make sure you don't fidget with your fingers. When you are asked your question, do NOT take the mic (unless you are told to do so) and begin your answer making eye contact with the person who asked it (usually the host or outgoing queen, whoever is holding the microphone). Then continue your answer by alternating your eye contact between each judge sitting in the audience. Then you also want to scan the audience to bring them into your answer. Finally, finish your answer by making eye contact with the person who asked the question. This process is pretty much just like the panel style interview. I cannot express how important it is to make eye contact with the judges while you are onstage. Looking over their heads will not have the same impact. Not being afraid to make eye contact shows confidence, so face your fears and just DO IT!

What I do when I'm coaching someone is to set up a mock interview. I also do my best to ensure that the judges

I bring in are ones that my client does not know. I give the mock judges score sheets, sample questions, and tell them they can also ask anything they want.

One woman I recently coached had a REALLY rough start during the first go around. She stumbled through her opening statement and the answers to her questions were just ok. She became EXTREMELY nervous with all the new faces in the room. Do you want this to happen to you in the ACTUAL interview? I think not.

After 2 or 3 rounds of practice, she was AMAZING! She went into the real interview with so much confidence that she knocked their socks off! She ended up placing 2nd Runner-up, which is an AMAZING accomplishment in this HIGHLY competitive state pageant. I was incredibly proud of her. I really think that her nerves may have gotten the best of her had I not set up the mock interview first.

If you don't have a coach, you can do this yourself. Gather some friends and family to be judges. Better yet...try to have someone gather mock judges for you that you don't know. The goal is to be a little uncomfortable (just like the real thing) and to ensure that they will give you unbiased feedback.

If you absolutely can't get anyone (or you just want extra rehearsal time), line up some stuffed animals on your couch and at least practice making eye contact. It sounds weird, but it works. Mark my words . . . I've done it.

Here is one final point that I REALLY want to talk about. Many coaches will tell you to answer questions regarding what you would do with the title by saying:

"As Miss/Mrs. _____ I **WILL** blah blah blah . . . "

I do NOT recommend doing that! I feel VERY strongly about this. I would rather have you say:

"As Miss/Mrs. _____ I **WOULD** blah blah blah . . . "

Coaches will tell you that saying I *will* shows confidence. I see their point, but I have also seen it backfire . . . badly. When I am a judge and someone says that to me, I feel like they are telling me how to do my job, by telling me who I am "supposed" to vote for, and I'm very put off.

You have to go into a pageant KNOWING that you can win, but it's another thing to TELL the judges that you already have. Does that make sense? By saying "I would" you are still telling the judges all the amazing things you would do with the title, but you are not forcing yourself on them.

If it came down to you (who said I "will") and another contestant (who said I "would") in the end, my vote would be for the one who wasn't pushy. I have seen an absolutely AMAZING contestant NOT advance further in the competition for a major title with this very issue.

As soon as the words came out of her mouth I went, "Uh oh . . . not good." And she didn't make the next cut. It was very sad as she could have easily won the whole thing. Ultimately you need to do what you think is best for you but keep my words in the back of your mind.

STATE COSTUME

This has always been one of my favorite areas of competition. It is usually not judged but it is still the first time the judges will see you onstage. In other words . . . you want to make a GREAT impression!

If a contestant that I am working with is on a budget (which I always was), I do not recommend breaking the bank on this as it is not judged. There are still ways of making a lasting impression without costing you a fortune. In other words . . . be creative! One of the most creative costumes I have ever seen was a woman who went as an Illinois Tollbooth. She had gray leggings (the road) with yellow lines going up and down. She was even wearing a basket to throw the quarters in (that's how we used to pay tolls)! It was creative, memorable and since she made it herself, it didn't cost her a lot of money.

You will always see women with spectacular costumes, especially on a national level. Just remember, you have to transport your costume to the city, state or country where your pageant is being held. If it's heavy, it will cost you quite a bit in excess baggage fees to get it there. You can ship it in advance, but that will also cost you. One of the ladies I competed with at a national pageant told me she paid $600 in excess baggage fees! *And* that was WITHOUT a heavy costume!

I also recommend that all your competition pieces are with you in your carry-on. Can you imagine if you spent thousands of dollars on your costume and the airline lost your bag??? The last time I flew to a national pageant I had

STATE COSTUME

my (very heavy) gown, interview dress, swimsuit, and costume in one garment bag. We rolled it up very carefully, so it didn't look too big to go through security. My husband guarded that thing with his LIFE as we went through the airport! Even if all my other bags got lost, I had the most important things with me.

Rehearsal clothes can most likely be purchased last minute in whatever city you are in and believe it or not, if your bags were to get lost, most contestants will be willing to lend you clothes as they probably brought too much anyway.

Another thing to consider is the cost of having it made. If you have the extra money or maybe a sponsor to cover the cost, by all means have your costume custom made. There are some amazing costume designers out there that can make something spectacular just for you and you will love it. You can also contact your pageant director. Maybe one of the former winners will rent out their costume or know someone who will. That is another affordable way of having a great costume at an affordable price.

My personal favorite way of obtaining your costume is to make it yourself. I made most of my costumes by myself or with my best friend Lisa. Here is a list of my costumes with a description:

Monarch Butterfly (Illinois state insect)—I bought some gold lamé fabric and cut out wings, trimmed them with black sequins, and attached them to a black leotard and dowel rods to hold in my hands. I wore black tights and found and antennae headband. It was basic but served its purpose. As it turned out, I was not the only monarch butterfly, but I was the ONLY one who introduced it as the state insect. In that respect . . . I stood out.

American Flag and Yellow Ribbon— This costume was the brainchild of my coach. It was a little farfetched, but it worked. I was showing my state's support for our troops during the Gulf War. I carried an American flag and wore a yellow ribbon around my neck. I also had a white top hat trimmed with red white and blue sequins. It was cute.

Chicago Bulls Cheerleader—I wanted to represent the Chicago Bulls as they were the HOT team at the time. My coach's daughter was a high school cheerleader (maybe poms (?); I don't remember) and she had a fantastic black and gold sequined costume. The bulls colors are, however, black and red. What I did was incorporate the color change into my introduction speech. I just said that my costume was black and GOLD since Michael Jordan and Scottie Pippen were GOING for the gold in this year's summer Olympics! Problem solved.

I also made a megaphone out of Styrofoam and covered the whole thing with individual sequins (you take a straight pin, stick it through a sequin, dip it in glue, and stick it in the Styrofoam, slightly overlapping so you don't see any white from the Styrofoam), in black and gold spelling out GO BULLS. I also bought some black pumps that were fabric and I made a gold sequin Nike stripe that I glued on with fabric glue. I really loved this costume!

Bugs Bunny—At the time of this pageant Bugs Bunny was the mascot for a large amusement park close to where I live. I made a *formal* costume out of a black tuxedo jacket, white tuxedo shirt sewed to purple swimsuit bottoms, a top hat with bunny ears coming out of the top and I made a sequin carrot the same way I made the megaphone. My speech said that I represented a day of all American family fun at Marriott's Great America.

Sailor Jack from Cracker Jack— This one took a little help. My husband's grandfather gave me his authentic WWII Navy Uniform top. I went to the Army/Navy Surplus Store and bought some bottoms. I also covered a sailor hat with iridescent white sequins. I bought some fabric that resem-  bled caramel corn and some friends from a department at work that painted logos on various equipment made the Cracker Jack sign and attached it to the fabric for me. It was

AMAZING and I couldn't have done it without them. FYI . . . Cracker Jack made its debut at the Columbian Exhibition in Chicago in 1893.

Abraham Lincoln—My costume for the Mrs. America Pageant was borrowed. One of our former winners had the most beautiful Abe Lincoln costume I had ever seen so I asked if I could borrow it. Easy Peasy.

Chicago Cubs—This is probably the costume that I am most proud of. My friend Lisa helped me bling a basic female baseball Halloween costume that had the right colors for the Cubs. I purchased an official Chicago Cubs Flag and hand-glued sequins covering the whole (very large) logo. It was VERY time consuming but was worth every minute. I also covered a red bat the same way, individually gluing red sequins covering the whole thing. When the stage lights hit these sequins it was spectacular! On a side note . . . . my Cubbies had a HISTORIC World Series win a few months later!

(*Unfortunately, due to permissions issue with MLB, we are unable to include a picture of the flag.*)

None of my costumes were very expensive, but they were all memorable. They may not have won any awards, but they made a good impression.

STATE COSTUME

Here are some ideas for costumes:
- State Bird
- State Tree
- State Insect (usually a butterfly)
- State Fish
- Famous building or structure
- Season (ex. Winter – Colorado . . . Summer—Arizona)
- Famous Person (ex. Walt Disney was born in Illinois so you could be a Disney Princess)
- Famous Restaurant (ex. McDonalds originated in Illinois)

And of course . . .

Sports Teams

A bit of advice for sports teams . . . don't just go out and buy a jersey and wear it with some leggings and high heels. That shows NO creativity and you will NOT stand out. Put some thought into it. Find some way of making it special. You want the judges to remember you ESPECIALLY since it is their first onstage impression of you.

    Here is another important thing to consider with your costume...your introduction speech. You want to tell the judges and audience about your costume, but you don't want to make it so long that you begin to fumble. This is a make it or break it moment for a lot of people. Your adrenaline will be HIGH, and you don't want to have a brain fart trying to remember a historical monologue about your costume. Make it short, sweet and to the point. That way you will sound confident:

"My name is Monica Skylling and I represent the LAND OF LINCOLN!"

This is a great time to break out your sewing and crafting skills. Maybe even make it a family project. If I was a judge and you told me that your kids and husband helped you make your costume, I would LOVE that no matter WHAT it looked like!

HAPPY CRAFTING!

SWIMSUIT/FITNESS WEAR

SWIMSUIT

This phase of competition scares a lot of contestants. You have to walk across the stage, possibly on national television in a swimsuit and 6-inch heels and look amazing doing it. Piece-of-cake, right? Not so fast . . . this preparation will start months in advance.

One thing that you have to keep in mind is that the judges aren't necessarily looking for the perfect body. They are looking for someone who is physically fit and leading a healthy lifestyle both physically and mentally. Having these traits will make you walk across that stage with confidence and the judges will take notice. I have seen several women win national pageants that did not have the most perfect body, maybe even a little extra weight, but they didn't let that stop them from strutting their stuff with amazing confidence. THAT is what the judges are looking for. I would like to think that pageants are becoming more and more accepting of a healthy body vs. one that is super skinny. I've seen more and more women make the Top 10 without their ribs sticking out and I think we are heading in the right direction. Only time will tell.

The first thing you want to do is develop a healthy eating plan. You do NOT want to starve yourself! Sadly, the joke of some pageant contestants eating only Tic-Tacs and egg whites to lose weight and stay thin is true. I cannot stress enough how bad this is for you. You will possibly develop an eating disorder and NO pageant is worth that! Find a good nutritionist if you need help and start meal prepping. If healthy food is easily accessible, you won't reach for the chips and chocolate (unless maybe your Aunt Dot is here for a visit).

Next, you want to develop some healthy training habits. Join a gym and try to get a trainer to sponsor you. Even if you don't meet with them every visit, they can at least teach you a good training routine. If you can't afford a gym, you can always workout at home. There are PLENTY of things you can do without any equipment. There are also trainers who will come to your home and help you develop a good routine.

Exercise bands are a wonderful way to develop some muscle definition without much cost and they take up literally no space at all. Invest in some bands and a yoga mat and hit YouTube. There are LOTS of free workout videos that you can work out with at home. It really can be done without an expensive gym membership. I did it myself in 1999.

Traditional

As far as the stage portion of this competition . . . have fun. You need to show some personality on stage, as well as confidence. The music should be upbeat, so it won't be hard to get that adrenaline flowing. You want a little bit of bounce in your step, but not too much. Your stance should either be the traditional pageant pose or the new modern pose with your legs slightly apart. You need to choose what works best for you and what makes your body look amazing. Some pageants may prefer that you only do the traditional pose if they are more conservative. Do your research.

When you are on that mark, that is your moment to shine. Do not rush. Take that moment to look each judge in the eyes, scan the audience, and then begin to make your exit. Keep that audience contact as long as you can with that beautiful smile on your face the whole time. Again . . . eye contact = confidence.

Modern

If your swimsuit is not provided, make sure you choose one that is right for YOU. Basically, if you don't feel confident in a two piece suit, get a one piece. It's that simple. I have seen plenty of women win national titles in a one piece swimsuit. It can be done. Your lack of confidence will show if you go with the two piece just because everyone else is probably going with a two piece.

As for the color . . . . keep it solid. Prints don't work well onstage as they can be very distracting. From a judge's point of view, I like to see bright colors. Something that will make you stand out. To this day, I still remember a contestant from the 1990s who wore this amazing lime green swimsuit. She had dark hair and her whole face lit up as soon as she stepped out on the stage. She made such an impression that I even remember her name! THAT is what I'm talking about.

Black or white is always a safe color choice but you won't be alone. Also, if you choose white, make sure it doesn't wash you out under the lights. Luckily, I could never wear white onstage because of my coloring so I never had to think about this, but what if you are onstage and you receive a SURPRISE visit from Aunt Flo? YIKES . . . TOO MUCH PRESSURE!

Interestingly enough, when you put a group of women together for a length of time, your cycles will start to align. When I was in Flight Attendant training, I had 3 roommates. Within a few weeks, we were all on the same cycle. It is a very strange phenomenon and can and will happen at a pageant, ESPECIALLY if you are at lengthy national one. You just do NOT want that happening to YOU when you are onstage, especially in a WHITE swimsuit!

When you are choosing the cut and style of your

swimsuit, it will be pretty obvious what looks good and what doesn't. Take a friend with you and make a day of it. You will find something perfect and that extra set of eyes will be very beneficial. Just make sure your friend is someone that will give you an HONEST opinion.

Your shoes with the swimsuit should be a nude color. Whatever color matches your skin tone the best. This is what will make your legs look longer and leaner. If you wear shoes that match your swimsuit, it will take away that effect.

I wore matching shoes for a photo shoot once, which was ok since it was not a judged event. I also wore them onstage back in the day before I knew better, but I would NEVER wear them onstage today.

Also, if you can walk in the platform, 6 inch type heels, then do it. They look FANTASTIC on stage. If you can't, then wear something high enough for you to feel comfortable. You also want to start wearing these at home *before* the pageant. Practice makes perfect, especially if you're not used to walking in heels that high. You also want to make sure you scuff them up a bit on the bottom, so you don't slip onstage.

If you have fair skin, get a spray tan! Those stage lights will wash you out like nobody's business. If you can't afford a tanning membership, maybe you can get a local tanning boutique to sponsor you. My husband and I actually purchased a tanning system online for WAY less than paying for a membership. That is also an option. My husband is very picky and gave me better spray tans than anyone else!

Keep your jewelry simple but remember . . . a little sparkle is always a good idea.

FITNESS WEAR

There isn't much difference from a swimsuit other than what you will be wearing onstage. Just make sure you follow the rules of the pageant you are competing in. If the rules state that your fitness wear shouldn't have any embellishments . . . don't put any on. If it says no high heeled sneakers . . . don't wear high heeled sneakers. Simply put, there are other ways of making yourself stand out rather than pushing the limits or breaking the rules.

Just like anything else, when you're choosing your fitness wear, choose something that makes you look and feel amazing. Short top . . . long top, short pants . . . long pants, whatever is best for YOU. Choose a flattering color, something that will pop onstage. You literally have endless options, just don't choose anything dull and flat. Bright colors are always a safe choice. If your pageant specifies white sneakers, wear white sneakers; otherwise having your shoes match your outfit would also be acceptable.

Your walk should have a little more pep than in swimsuit, and of course, still show lots of personality. Just like before, when you hit your mark onstage, don't rush. Take that moment and make eye contact with the judges and scan the audience. This is your time to shine, don't waste it by rushing through.

Some people prefer swimsuit, and some prefer fitness wear. This is when researching a pageant is important. I personally prefer swimsuit so when I'm doing my research, that is something I look for. I wouldn't necessarily turn down an opportunity because the pageant had fitness wear, but it may sway my decision. This is a very personal choice and neither one is wrong. Just choose what is best for you.

One last thing regarding swimsuit OR fitness wear . . . and this is a little sensitive . . . there's no nice way of putting this . . . so I'll just say it . . . CAMEL TOE! (If you don't know what this is, it's a front wedgie.) If your anatomy is such that you tend to have this issue, the solution is simple . . . pop a panty liner in your swimsuit/fitness wear and you're good to go!

EVENING GOWN

I LOVE THE EVENING GOWN COMPETITION!

This is where you can show class, elegance, and individuality. Choosing the perfect gown can either be easy or it may take a while to find. Make sure to give yourself plenty of time to find the perfect one because this is NOT the time to settle!

Gowns can either be affordable, very VERY expensive, or somewhere in between. If you can find a sponsor to donate or lend you a gown, DO IT! If not, just find the best one you can in your price range. If you have any sponsors donate money, you can always put it towards the gown. I had a sponsor once who donated money and was insistent on it going toward the gown. When he watched the pageant and saw me onstage in *his* gown, he knew that he had played a very important role in my journey.

The perfect gown is a very individual decision. It can be

flashy or plain, high cut or low cut, colorful or simple. This is another time where your options are endless. I would recommend something that accentuates your features, makes your face light up on that stage and most important . . . makes you feel like a QUEEN.

Over many, many years there has been a trend of winners wearing white. I'm glad to see that this trend seems to be fading away. Many people can't wear white because of their coloring so seeing many winners today in bold colors makes me very happy. Choose something original, something you don't think a lot of other women will wear. The judges may remember the girl in the fuchsia dress over the one (of MANY) in black. If you don't want to wear a bold color, it is really ok. Black, white or champagne will never go out of style and is always classy. It is up to you how bold you want to be. You can always dress up a plain color with jewelry or maybe a cape. Pretty much anything goes here, as long as the dress is full length. Just remember that if you chose a "safe" color and someone has either the exact same gown or one that is similar, it will look DIFFERENT on both of you! Do NOT let this sway your confidence!

That brings up another subject. If you borrow a gown, make sure it fits properly. If it is too short or too long, you will not look put together. Part of what the judges are looking for is that you choose a gown that is suitable for you and your body type . . . not the price tag. Borrowing a gown is perfectly fine but you may need to have it tacked up or down, in or out to make it fit properly. Just make sure everything can be easily let out after the pageant when it's time to return it.

Another bit of great advice . . . . please for the love of all that is holy CUT OFF THE LOOPIE THINGS! I can't tell you how many women I have seen go out onstage with those loops sticking out of their gown. It looks nothing short of tacky. You can always safety pin them back in to transport your gown, but this way you won't run the risk of them sticking out.

Some gowns need jewelry, and some do not. If your gown has a busy bodice, I would suggest not wearing a necklace. If your gown is simpler, a statement necklace would look amazing. Big bold earrings are also a must in most cases. If you chose to wear a bracelet, make sure it won't snag the fabric. You definitely don't want to have any nicks or pulls, especially if it is loaned to you.

As far as shoes go, you really don't need to purchase anything extra. Your nude-colored swimsuit shoes should work just fine; then you will, of course, have less to think about backstage. If you choose to have specific evening gown shoes, that is of course ok as well. Just make sure they flatter your gown if they are visible.

Some women will choose to put their hair up for evening gown competition. I really don't recommend doing this. One contestant that I saw at a national pageant had this AMAZING hair. It was different and unique, and it made her stand out from the other women. When she came out in evening gown with her hair up, I didn't even recognize her. She was easily the front runner, but by putting her hair up, she quickly took herself OUT of the running and didn't even make the next cut. Of course there are women who win even though they put their hair up, I'm just saying that it is risky. What if they judges remember you as the girl with the AMAZING natural hair, or chic bob and then all of a sudden the hair is gone, and they don't recognize you? Judging is QUICK! You don't want them spending most of that time trying to place who you are. The choice is ultimately up to you, but you are definitely taking a risk.

As far as your walk goes . . . take your time! This is not a time to be bouncy and upbeat. You should be gracefully gliding across that stage exuding elegance. As always, make eye contact with the judges and scan the audience. Your pose should be anything you feel looks best with your gown. Arms at your side, one hand on the hip, two hands on the hip. Whatever accentuates your figure. If you have a coach they will help you decide, or you can have someone take pictures of you and you will make the right choice.

If at all possible, try your gown out on a stage under stage lighting. Maybe someone at a local high school or community theater can help you with this. I have seen several women come out on stage and their gown is either totally see through or it doesn't flow while walking and they're constantly tripping over it. Give it a trial run first just to make sure.

Whatever gown you choose . . . just OWN IT! This could possibly be the most beautiful you have ever felt. ENJOY the moment!

MISCELLANEOUS TIPS

The number of tips I can give you is about as endless as your choices for a gown. So as not to overwhelm you, here are some important ones.

GETTING SPONSORS

Sponsors are basically purchasing advertising space by giving you money or products. Most pageants will have an ad page with your photo and title, and this is where you place your sponsor ads for their business. My rule of thumb is that the more money or products they donate, the bigger ad they get. If it's a family member or friend giving you money, a nice thank you and shout out on the ad page would suffice. Contact anyone and everyone you know who owns a business such as:

- Lawyers
- Salon owners
- Restaurant owners
- Doctors' offices
- Dress shops
- Boutiques
- Car dealers
- Banks

Really, anyone you can think of. If you know them personally, great. You can just ask. What I used to do, however is to get dressed up, hair and make-up done and just walk into various businesses with some photos and information on the pageant. This is how I funded my competitions when I was younger. I was determined to not spend too much out of pocket, and I was not shy about asking. You have to go in there with confidence. This really is a great advertising opportunity for local businesses. Hundreds if not thousands of people will see this ad page, so in those terms, the cost is minimal to them. You can also pay them back by making an appearance. Maybe they have a function where you could be there signing photos and taking pictures with their customers. This would be great exposure for you as well.

I have included a sample of the information sheet at the end of this chapter that I would bring to prospective sponsors. Feel free to use the same one or tweak it to fit your individual needs.

One thing you DEFINITELY want to keep in mind is that your sponsors have to be AWARE that they are a sponsor. I know that sounds weird, but here is what happened to me once. I was coaching a woman who was a contestant in a large state pageant. Without my knowledge, she listed me as a sponsor in her ad page in the program book. I was FURIOUS! As a coach, I would not feel right sponsoring one client and not another, so to be fair, I don't sponsor anyone. She took it upon herself to put my name down without my consent. Could you imagine how it would feel to another contestant that I was coaching in the same pageant if she would have seen this? She would have felt that I was playing favorites and that is not something a coach should do. Just keep that in mind.

AD PAGE

Some pageants will have a printer design everyone's ad page so they all look similar. You would just have to submit your sponsor information. Other pageants will have you design your own. You always have the option of using someone that specializes in this, but you will run the risk of not having one that stands out. You ultimately want your ad to jump off the page. During my preparation for a recent pageant, I contacted a printer that specialized in designing ad pages. I thought I would save some time by doing it this way. I had a very specific vision of what I wanted my ad page to look like and when I shared it with him, he refused to do it. He said it would look messy. Of course he had NO WAY of seeing inside my head, that it wouldn't be messy AT ALL, so I thanked him for his time and paid my computer savvy son to do it for me and I absolutely LOVED how it turned out! It was EXACTLY what I wanted.

I have included a copy (with some fake sponsors) to give you an idea. Your pageant director may possibly send you some examples as well. Just remember . . . as with anything else, you want to STAND OUT!

PHOTOS

I know I've touched on this before, but it is VERY important to have an AMAZING headshot! You will need to find a photographer that specializes in pageant photos. If you go to just anybody, it could end up looking like a school photo and you don't want that. I have also seen contestants send in a selfie. Yes . . . it has happened. You DEFINITELY don't want to do that! There are other areas where you can cut costs, but don't do it with your photos. Hire a professional as well as a reputable hair and make-up artist and choose a photo that LOOKS LIKE YOU! Your photo is literally the first time a judge will see what you look like. Make it count, but also make sure they recognize you when you walk into the interview.

    Another helpful tip for the photo shoot...wear something that buttons or zips and does NOT go over your head! You don't want to have someone spend all that time doing your hair and then have you mess it up by pulling your shirt over your head. Also, bring lots of wardrobe and jewelry choices. When I say lots, I mean LOTS! Your photographer and/or hair and make-up artist will go through what you brought and choose something that will look great on camera. You want to give them a lot to pick from. Bring different colors and necklines. If you are only getting a headshot, you don't need to worry about what you wear on the bottom (so just be comfortable). What I do is to purchase MANY options to bring with me, leave the tags on and then return whatever is NOT used. It's an affordable way to bring an amazing wardrobe without having to fork out all the bucks of keeping all these items.

STAGE HAIR AND MAKE-UP

This again will be a personal choice. Stage make-up is very different from everyday make-up and a professional make-up artist will know the difference. They are, however, very costly. If you have the funds, it is a great way to take some of the pressure off of you. Just make sure you have a trial run if possible. You don't want to be unhappy with their work when there is no time to correct it.

You can also learn how to do it yourself. Maybe the make-up artist at your photo shoot can give you some tips. Otherwise there is always YouTube. There are SOOOOOOO many make-up tutorials out there! Have fun and practice. Just make sure the brand of make-up you choose to use will hold up under the stage lighting.

You also have to remember that since stage lighting can cut right through your make-up, you really have to pack it on. My trainer used to tell me that if you don't look like a streetwalker, your make-up isn't dark enough. This is actually kind of true!

The same thing goes for your hair. Maybe your stylist could train you how to do your hair. If not . . . hit YouTube and practice, practice, practice.

GETTING TO THE LOCATION

No matter if your pageant is at a hotel or theater, if you fly or drive, GET THERE EARLY! I can't possibly stress this enough. What if you have car trouble? Or what if your flight is cancelled? What if the airline loses your luggage? The *what if's* are endless, but my point is to be prepared for anything and you'll be ok, as long as you don't arrive at the last minute. Arriving late will just stress you out. What if the private interviews are held right after arrival? Do you want to be a total stress ball during your interview because you didn't get there on time? I think not. I always recommend getting there at LEAST the day before.

WHAT TO BRING BACKSTAGE

I will be including a packing list for you to use as far as what to bring with you to your competition, but you don't have to bring everything with you backstage.

Here are some basic things you will need:

- ❏ Competition wardrobe
- ❏ Make-up
- ❏ Hair products
- ❏ Jewelry
- ❏ Medicine
- ❏ Sewing kit
- ❏ Vaseline
- ❏ Snacks
- ❏ Water
- ❏ Butt spray (for swimsuit competition)
- ❏ Permanent marker
- ❏ Masking tape
- ❏ Panty liners

Again, I will include a more detailed packing list later but those are a few key things you should have with you. Snacks are very important. You probably haven't been eating well and if you get lightheaded, you'll want to pop some protein to feel better quickly so you don't faint onstage. Just make sure they aren't messy. Even just a bag of M & M's would help (as long as no one has a nut allergy) or maybe a cheese stick. Also make sure you sip water. You don't want to be dehydrated which can also make you faint. Just make sure you don't drink too much and have to pee all the time. At one pageant, I had to go REALLY bad right before the evening gown competition. I put my gown on as fast as I could and ran to the bathroom. All of a sudden I hear a SPLAT as I accidentally dropped my gown in the toilet! NOT GOOD! Luckily, you couldn't really see anything, but if this happens to you, pee BEFORE you put your gown on!

Another good tip is to have a small pop-up hamper with you. You do NOT have time between numbers to be neatly hanging your garments and putting away your jewelry. If you have a hamper you can just drop your things in there as you're changing and hang them up later when you have time. The changes are VERY quick and there will probably be someone the dressing room yelling,

"LET'S GO LADIES . . ."

Make sure you label EVERYTHING. If someone takes something of yours by mistake (or "by mistake") you want to be able to prove that it's yours. Also, many women will have similar items, such as shoes. You want to make sure YOU aren't taking something by mistake! It's very easy to get things mixed up backstage. If your area isn't already marked, you can just slap on a piece of masking tape and mark your territory.

Try your best to have everything you might need. If you forget something don't worry, just ask a chaperone. Chances are they will have it in their bag of goodies. Just don't forget your WARDROBE!

MISCELLANEOUS TIPS

PAGEANT BINDER

You want to make sure you have a binder with you that contains your application, judges bio, opening statement speech, signed contracts, some interview questions, hotel confirmation, airline confirmation basically anything important you might need. This way it will all be in one place.

You also want to make sure you look over your judges bio before you go into your interview, that way all the information you put down will be fresh in your mind. Having it in a binder will give you easy access and you won't have to look for it.

AUTOGRAPH CARDS

If you won a state or national title, your director may supply these for you. If not, make your own. It is not that expensive and well worth the cost even if you have a small, local title. People LOVE to get autographs, especially kids. If you have an appearance in your hometown, wouldn't it be nice to have pictures to sign for those who ask? It is also another way to get your name out in your community.

Mrs. Illinois-America 1999
Monica Skylling
3rd Runner-Up to Mrs. America

Your sponsors will also most likely display them at their place of business. All you need is a photo, preferably in your crown and your name and title listed below. You can design it on your home computer, and have it printed at your local printer. Maybe they'll even sponsor you with free cards. You won't know unless you ask.

SOCIAL MEDIA

One thing that I would like to stress is that whether it is your ad page, autograph cards, or especially social media . . . USE YOUR FULL TITLE!

It would not be fair to the pageant that I am representing to just write:

Mrs. Illinois 1999

You need to specify what pageant system you are a titleholder for:

Mrs. Illinois-America 1999

Mrs. Illinois-United States 2016

Mrs. Illinois-International 2017

This is actually a **BIG DEAL,** so just play it safe and put your whole title on EVERYTHING!

MISCELLANEOUS TIPS

MISS/MRS. _____
USA/AMERICA... 2019

Monica Skylling

*** Say something nice about your pageant here ***

· **YOU can be a sponsor by supporting** ·
Miss/Mrs. _____ (USA/America...) 2019

Sponsorship levels are as follows:

PLATINUM: $1000
- Large ad with logo in National Program Book
- Use of Monica's photo for business promotions naming you as a proud sponsor

GOLD: $500
- Ad with logo in National Program Book
- Use of Monica's photo for business promotions naming you as a proud sponsor

SILVER: $250
- Listing in National Program Book as a sponsor
- Use of Monica's photo for business promotions naming you as a proud sponsor

BRONZE: $100
- Honorable Mention in National Program Book
- Use of Monica's photo for business promotions naming you as a proud sponsor

Sponsorships larger than $1000 can be negotiated as well as services or products equivalent of any value

Appearances are negotiable for any sponsorship level of Silver, Gold or Platinum
(Photo signing, trade shows, emcee for event...)

"I am VERY proud to be representing my home state in the Miss/Mrs. _____ Pageant! As Miss/Mrs. _____ 2019, I will be continuing my current volunteer work with Domestic Violence Awareness as well as MANY other community events"!   ~Monica

PACKING LIST

Having a good packing list is EXTREMELY important! You will certainly be feeling a bit overwhelmed which could easily make you forget something.

Here is a list that I have put together, but feel free to add things that are personal to you.

PACKING LIST

- ____ Interview outfit
- ____ State costume (if needed)
- ____ Competition swimsuit/fitness wear
- ____ Evening gown
- ____ Nude shoes for swimsuit
- ____ White sneakers for fitness wear
- ____ Evening gown shoes (if needed)
- ____ Interview shoes
- ____ Rehearsal shoes
- ____ Flip flops or sandals
- ____ Jewelry
- ____ Accessories
- ____ Swimsuit for swimming (not your competition suit)
- ____ Heavy duty garment bag for gown
- ____ Clear garment bags to organize your outfits
- ____ Zip-Loc bags
- ____ Rehearsal clothes

PACKING LIST

____ Outfit to wear to and from the theater that doesn't go over your head
____ Pantyhose (if needed)
____ Sleep wear
____ Sweater for the cold theater during rehearsals
____ Under garments
____ Incidental money
____ Alarm clock(s)
____ Iron/steamer
____ Toothbrush and toothpaste
____ Mouthwash
____ Deodorant/Anti-Perspirant
____ Cosmetics
____ Hairbrush
____ Hair accessories
____ Hairspray
____ Vaseline
____ Shampoo
____ Conditioner
____ Curling iron
____ Flat iron
____ Blow dryer
____ Rollers
____ Make-up mirror
____ Lashes
____ Lash glue
____ Nail file

- ____ Nail polish for touch ups
- ____ Nail glue
- ____ Press on nails for emergency repair
- ____ Razor
- ____ Tweezers
- ____ Glasses
- ____ Self-tanner
- ____ Contact lenses and solution
- ____ Sewing kit
- ____ Safety pins
- ____ Body creams and lotions
- ____ Tampons
- ____ Panty liners
- ____ Personal medications
- ____ Pain killers
- ____ Anti-diarrheal (Pageant diarrhea is REAL!)
- ____ Laxatives
- ____ Antacids
- ____ Allergy medicine
- ____ Cortisone cream
- ____ Kleenex
- ____ Q-tips
- ____ Band-Aids
- ____ Baby wipes
- ____ Masking tape
- ____ Permanent marker
- ____ Pen

PACKING LIST

- ____ Scissors
- ____ Butt spray
- ____ Umbrella
- ____ Copies of paperwork
- ____ Pageant binder
- ____ Snacks
- ____ Good luck charms
- ____ Garment rack (NEVER enough hanging space for 2 contestants if you share a room)
- ____ Extension cord
- ____ Water
- ____ Preparation-H
- ____
- ____
- ____
- ____
- ____
- ____
- ____

    This is obviously a very extensive list. You don't need to bring everything on it, just what pertains to you. I have also left space to add items that are specific to you.

    Just remember . . . it is better to pack too much and not need it then to forget something you need at home.

IN CLOSING

THANK YOU SO MUCH FOR READING my story. I certainly hope that the things I have learned during my pageant journey will in turn help you in yours.

Pageants are an amazing way to learn things you will take with you for the rest of your life. You will never again be afraid of a job interview. NONE of them are as intimidating as a pageant interview (except maybe a Flight Attendant interview).

Because of the supportive nature of the sisterhood, you will often find yourself complementing complete strangers . . . and you will make their day. Pageantry is a very unique world. During competition you will be giving and receiving compliments, sometimes strange compliments on a regular basis.

My roommate at a national pageant came up to me one day and very genuinely said: "WOW . . . Your boobs look GREAT in that dress." And she meant it! I wouldn't recommend saying that to a stranger, but in the pageant world it is A-OK!

You will also make friends . . . GOOD friends. Friends that will pick you up when you are down, tell you you're beautiful when you're having a fat, bad hair day. Friends that will always support you because they understand how important support is. These are women who are not afraid or intimidated by you and genuinely want to see you succeed. They will do anything and everything in their power to help you achieve your goals because they are goal oriented themselves. As with everything in life, you will come across some bad eggs, but they are few and far between. The women (and men) you will meet are the ones who will straighten your crown, whether it is real or invisible.

I am so thankful for the opportunities that have been given to me through pageantry. I am proud and honored to still be part of this crazy, amazing world for over 30 years.

If you could only take away one thing from this book it is this . . . you are ENOUGH! No one can be a better you than YOU. I said it before but just remember, there will always be someone taller than you, thinner than you and prettier than you, but they are NOT you. If you go into competition as prepared as you can possibly be and do the best that you can possibly do, the growth you will make in your personal development will be invaluable.

Dreams do not have an expiration date. No matter how old you are, it is time to live life to the fullest and remember . . . don't let anyone dull your sparkle, because sparkles are where dreams are made!

Monica

About the Author . . .

MONICA SKYLLING has been involved in the pageant/entertainment industry for over 30 years. Her extensive pageant background is what has inspired her to write her first book, *Confessions of an Aging Beauty Queen*. The trials and tribulations as well as behind the scenes action truly makes pageantry a world of its own. Through her words, everyone can now get a glimpse of the glitz, glamour and dedicated hard work that it takes to win that crown.

Her modeling and acting credits range from various training and ad campaigns for United Airlines to being a St. Pauli Girl. Monica loves the stage and along with performing in several plays and musicals, she is also a graduate of Chicago's Second City and has performed on the same stage that so many Saturday Night Live Alumni got their start.

Her passion for pageantry is obvious and she has many titles under her belt. Her favorite would have to be Mrs.

Illinois-America 1999 and later placing as 3rd Runner-Up to Mrs. America! She has also worked for many years as a pageant coach, judge and coordinator and doesn't see herself stopping anytime soon.

As well as acting and modeling, Monica currently works full time as a Flight Attendant for American Airlines and lives in the northern suburbs of Illinois with her family.

www.Facebook.com/MonicaSkylling

www.Instagram.com @MonicaSkylling

email: MonicaSkylling@gmail.com

www.ingramcontent.com/pod-product-compliance
Lightning Source LLC
Chambersburg PA
CBHW061218070526
44584CB00029B/3889